Fighting Ghosts and Chasing the Wind:

The Hero of Tal Afar

MG Najim al-Jubouri

Craig Lancto

Second Edition

Good Gnus Press

Shenandoah, Virginia

ISBN-13: 9781080382972

DEDICATION

This book is dedicated to Col. Bill Turner, USA (ret.), a model of integrity and professionalism.

CONTENTS

"A hero to the people of Tal Afar and Iraq"

"Mayor of Tal Afar Najim Al Jubouri--the hero of President Bush's March 20 speech in Cleveland--is a rare leader in a country fraught with fear and uncertainty. His strong leadership, both as chief of police and mayor, helped clean up this city of a quarter-million people in northwest Iraq when it was overrun by terrorists and suffering from a decrepit infrastructure. He helped reform the police by making them more representative and accountable. He worked diligently with Coalition Forces and Iraqi Security Forces on counterinsurgency efforts in September 2005."

"Najim Al Jubouri is without a doubt a rare and brave leader, and a hero to the people of Tal Afar and Iraq."

U.S. Ambassador Cameron Munter,

Leader of the Provincial Reconstruction Team in Nineveh,

2006

Preface

In April 2015, Iraqi Prime Minister Haider al Abadi named Major General Najim al-Jubouri commander of Nineveh operations, the forces battling to liberate Nineveh Province. Again.

This time the fight is against DAESH (also known as ISIL or ISIS, the band of extremists fighting to establish a Muslim caliphate, through means and methods abhorrent to observant and faithful Muslims and the rest of the civilized world). Not even ten years before, Najim was successfully fighting the same battle against a different enemy: al-Qaeda, then the primary scourge of the Middle East, now a warm memory compared to DAESH (an acronym for Dawlat al-Islamiyya fi al-Iraq wa al-Shiam). I prefer the term "DAESH" to "Islamic State in the Levant" or "Islamic State in Syria and Iraq" because members of that terrorist gang consider it insulting.

Coordinating with the American-led Coalition Forces, Najim fought and won the battle against al-Qaeda when he was both mayor and chief of police in Tal Afar, the second (to Mosul) largest city in Nineveh Province. In a joint operation and against great odds and common sense, Iraqi and Coalition Forces went door to door, block by block, clearing al-Qaeda and their arms caches from the city that had been their safe haven and center of operations. It was a technique that Najim learned in al-Basra as a young intelligence officer in 1991.

Between sweeping terrorists out of Tal Afar and taking up the fight against DAESH, Najim—whom American Ambassador Cameron Munter, first leader of the Nineveh Provincial Reconstruction Team termed the "Hero of Tal Afar"—and his family have been living in exile in the Metropolitan Washington area, unable to return to Iraq, under threat of death. After President (G.W.) Bush publicly praised him in a speech, al-Qaeda put a price on his head, his body armor stopped an assassin's bullet, his house was blown up, and his family moved to Kurdistan. American friends, particularly Colonel (later, Lieutenant General) H.R. McMaster, who would become National Security Advisor to President Donald Trump in 2017, arranged for Najim and his family to flee to the United States.

General McMaster also helped to secure Najim's position as a distinguished researcher at the Near East South Asia Center for Strategic Studies, a Department of Defense organization dedicated to bringing together elected and military leaders from Asia and the Near East to seek better understanding and possible solutions to the panoply of issues facing the region.

General McMaster, a loyal friend and ally, drove from Norfolk, Virginia, to Washington, D.C., to support Najim in each of his hearings when he was seeking refugee status.

In Northern Virginia, Najim's family found a comfortable suburban life with food that was plentiful and much less expensive than that in Iraq—when it could be found. Their home was a modest American home, and Najim enjoyed barbecuing in his yard. After high school, his younger son joined the U.S. Army.

But his country needed him again.

At this writing, in April 2016, Major General al Jubouri and his troops are poised to recapture Mosul, from DAESH, which has terrorized residents and confiscated their food, possessions, homes, wives, and daughters.

Most of the material here is what Najim or other eye-witnesses, including U.S. military officers who served with Najim in Tal Afar, reported to me over several years and many (delectable) meals at his home. Much is in his own words, or at least what I understood to be his meaning in conversations that sometimes faltered in a search for the right word or a reasonable facsimile thereof. We relied heavily on an Arabic-English app. The narrative is not strictly linear; it reflects Najim's train of thought as he recalled the events these many years later. Sometimes minor facts are seemingly contradictory as is often the case in relying on memory instead of recorded notes. It is essentially a personal recollection, and subject to the vagaries of memory, especially when related to stressful circumstances. Deficiencies are the result of my imperfect understanding of the fascinating story that MG al Jubouri was relating to me.

CL

Foreword

It has been my lot to be present at times and places that history has proven to be far more significant than they seemed at the time.

It has nothing to do with foresight or brilliance or personal decisions, so much as the convergence of events and the chemistry and goals of the characters who played such significant roles.

This is the story of an Iraqi Air Defense officer who saw the destruction that Coalition Forces visited upon his country under Saddam Hussein, whose destiny would include becoming police chief and the mayor of the lawless, ancient, and venerable city of Tal Afar in the north of Iraq at the very time that that city became pivotal in the peaceful resolution of hostilities sought by Coalition Forces.

This is a book about Iraq, Iraqi people, Iraqi culture, and the ravages visited upon them. It is a book about turning enmity to friendship and destruction to reconstruction. It is about turning defeat to victory...and it is about an Iraqi patriot forced into exile.

The characters in this story include men and women, Iraqis and Americans, military and civilians who paved the route to democracy and harmony amid destruction and despair. It is a story about these disparate characters learning to trust each other and to work as a team towards peaceful resolution in a troubled and turbulent region.

It is about building bridges between peoples, cultures, and nations.

~~~~

The story of Tal Afar in the biblical province of Nineveh is a model of solidarity and cooperation among former enemies. The paradigm that we relied on—clear, hold, and build—in that city served as a guide for how to proceed in insurgent-held cities throughout Iraq. The success in Tal Afar relied heavily on men and women,

American and Iraqi, willing to work to understand each other's cultures, religions, and customs.

Despite the common misconception of many, if not most, Westerners, the Arab world not only lacks homogeneity, but it sustains vigorous rival factions, theocratic foes within what Westerners often consider the monolithic world of Islam.

Although they follow the same basic religious tenets, Western Muslims are not typically the same as Middle Eastern Muslims; Muslims in Saudi Arabia are not the same as Muslims in Morocco or Indonesia. Shi'a Muslims are not Sunni Muslims, and the rift is deeper than the historic argument about the legitimate heir to the Prophet. Religious sects within Islam are at each other's throats, engaging in a tradition of fierce, although sometimes concealed, enmity.

Many Iraqis harbor ill-will against the Kurdish and Turkmen Muslims who live among them, and depending on the locale, women are treated as men's equals, hold public office, and positions of power, or are bereft of rights, covered by burqas and hijabs, and forbidden to drive a car or walk on the street without being accompanied by a close male relative. Westerners, who frequently conflate Arabs and Muslims although one is not always the other, often perceive those who live in the Middle East as barbarians, or, at best, as quaint folk, backward in their ways, the contemporary iteration of the "white man's burden."

Despite the generally good advice on the subject that the U.S. Army has promulgated to its troops at least since World War II, if I were to point to the one error, the single misstep that has prolonged and exacerbated Western intervention in the Middle East, it would be ignorance. Maybe worse than ignorance is the benign contempt, the hubristic conceit that these barbarians are not worth consideration as equals, that they are beneath any effort to understand them and their culture.

A second, but corollary, error is that Americans—the Coalition Forces—never saw Iraqis as people in their own right. They saw only a two-dimensional enemy, a conquered people. Westerners— especially I think Americans—view other countries from their own perspective, without considering or caring about what the locals think. They do not see people struggling to survive, praying for peace in their lives. Their tunnel vision cost them the goodwill of the people they ostensibly were there to help, to elevate, to free from the bloody tyranny of Saddam Hussein, viewed solely as the caricature of a villainous tyrant or the personification of evil.

The key to winning the hearts and minds of the Iraqi people was first to see them as fellow citizens of the world and then to treat them with humanity, not to enter as conquering heroes, as victors. The Iraqi people were not—are not—enemies of the United States or the Coalition writ large. They did not pick a fight with America, yet they often were treated as aggressors. Until those lessons were learned, Americans would continue fighting ghosts and chasing the wind.

As has been true down through history, a few courageous and foresighted men and women broke the pattern. They understood that making allies of the Iraqi people deprived the insurgents of their power, their allies, and their sanctuary. To alienate the Iraqi people was to drive them into the arms of terrorists and the enemies of democracy; to win their loyalty was to earn devoted friends and lifetime allies.

The key to enduring victory—at least until a new and more powerful adversary was allowed to take root and flourish—was to turn the Iraqis' mistrust and hatred of the swaggering American victors to a willing alliance with their liberators who would help them to learn democracy.

A lesson for the Americans was that human casualties were not collateral damage. They were loved ones—fathers, mothers, sons, and brothers—killed, injured, or disfigured, by the war that no one wanted, waged between the Americans and Iraq...or, as often, between and among Iraqis.

Najim Abdullah al-Jubouri

Overview
George W. Bush

"By September 2004, the terrorists and insurgents had basically seized control of Tal Afar."

President George W. Bush

In a speech to the City Club of Cleveland, Ohio, on March 20, 2006, President George W. Bush provided a concise description of the situation that existed and events that transpired in the city of Tal Afar in Nineveh Province in northern Iraq. In this excerpt from that speech, he lauded Najim al-Jubouri's role in ridding Tal Afar of the oppressive domination of al-Qaeda:

Focus on Iraq

I'm going to tell you the story of a northern Iraqi city called Tal Afar, which was once a key base of operations for al-Qaeda and is today a free city that gives reason for hope for a free Iraq.

Tal Afar is a city of more than 200,000 residents, roughly the population of Akron, Ohio. In many ways, Tal Afar is a microcosm of Iraq: It has dozens of tribes of different ethnicity and religion. Most of the city residents are Sunnis of Turkmen origin. Tal Afar sits just 35 miles from the Syrian border. It was a strategic location for al-Qaeda and their leader, [Abu Musab al-] Zarqawi. Now, it's important to remember what al-Qaeda has told us, their stated objectives. Their goal is to drive us out of Iraq so they can take the country over. Their goal is to overthrow moderate Muslim governments throughout the region. Their goal is to use Iraq as a base from which to launch attacks against America. To achieve this goal, they're recruiting terrorists from the Middle East to come into Iraq to infiltrate its cities, and to sow violence and destruction so that no legitimate government can exercise control. And Tal Afar was a key way station for their operations in Iraq.

After we removed Saddam Hussein in April 2003, the terrorists began moving into the city. They sought to divide Tal Afar's many ethnic and religious groups, and forged an alliance of convenience with those who benefited from Saddam's regime and others with their own grievances. They skillfully used propaganda to foment hostility toward the coalition and the new Iraqi government. They exploited a weak economy to recruit young men to their cause. And by September 2004, the terrorists and insurgents had basically seized control of Tal Afar.

We recognized the situation was unacceptable. So we launched a military operation against them. After three days of heavy fighting, the terrorists and the insurgents fled the city. Our strategy at the time was to stay after the terrorists and keep them on the run. So coalition forces kept moving, kept pursuing the enemy and routing out the terrorists in other parts of Iraq.

Unfortunately, in 2004 the local security forces there in Tal Afar weren't able to maintain order, and so the terrorists and the insurgents eventually moved back into the town. Because the terrorists threatened to murder the families of Tal Afar's police, its members rarely ventured out from the headquarters in an old Ottoman fortress. The terrorists also took over local mosques, forcing local imams out and insisting that the terrorist message of hatred and intolerance and violence be spread from the mosques. The same happened in Tal Afar's schools, where the terrorists eliminated real education and instead indoctrinated young men in their hateful ideology. By November 2004, two months after our operation to clear the city, the terrorists had returned to continue their brutal campaign of intimidation.

The return of al-Qaeda meant the innocent civilians in Tal Afar were in a difficult position. Just put yourself in the shoes of the citizens of Tal Afar as all this was happening. On the one side, you hear coalition and Iraqi forces saying they're coming to protect you -- but they'd already come in once, and they had not stopped the terrorists from coming back. You worry that when the coalition goes after the terrorists, you or your family may be caught in the crossfire, and your city might be destroyed. You don't trust the police. You badly want to believe the coalition forces really can help you out, but three decades of Saddam's brutal rule have taught you a lesson: Don't stick your neck out for anybody.

On the other side, you see the terrorists and the insurgents. You know they mean business. They control the only hospital in town. You see that the mayor and other political figures are collaborating with the terrorists. You see how the people who worked as interpreters for the coalition forces are beheaded. You see a popular city councilman gunned down in front of his horrified wife and children. You see a respected Sheikh and an Imam kidnapped and murdered. You see the terrorists deliberately firing mortars into playgrounds and soccer fields filled with children. You see communities becoming armed enclaves. If you are in a part of Tal Afar that was not considered friendly, you see that the terrorists cut off your basic services like electricity and water. You and your family feel besieged and you see no way out.

The savagery of the terrorists and insurgents who controlled Tal Afar is really hard for Americans to imagine. They enforced their rule through fear and intimidation -- and women and children were not spared. In one grim incident, the terrorists kidnapped a young boy from the hospital and killed him. And then they booby-trapped his body and placed him along a road where his family would see him. And when the boy's father came to retrieve his son's body, he was blown up. These weren't random acts of violence; these were deliberate and highly-organized attempts to maintain control through intimidation. In Tal Afar, the terrorists had schools for kidnapping and beheading and laying IEDs. And they sent a clear message to the citizens of the city: Anyone who dares oppose their reign of terror will be murdered.

As they enforced their rule by targeting civilians, they also preyed upon adolescents craving affirmation. Our troops found one Iraqi teenager who was taken from his family by the terrorists. The terrorists routinely abused him and violated his dignity. The terrorists offered him a chance to prove his manhood -- by holding the legs of captives as they were beheaded. When our forces interviewed this boy, he told them that his greatest aspiration was to be promoted to the killer who would behead the bound captives. al-Qaeda's idea of manhood may be fanatical and perverse, but it served two clear purposes: It helped provide recruits willing to commit any atrocity, and it enforced the rule of fear.

The result of this barbarity was a city where normal life had virtually ceased. Colonel H.R. McMaster of the Third Armored Cavalry Regiment described it this way: "When you come into a place in the grip of al-Qaeda, you see a ghost town. There are no children playing in the streets. Shops are closed and boarded. All construction is stopped. People stay inside, prisoners in their own homes." This is the brutal reality that al-Qaeda wishes to impose on all the people of Iraq.

The ability of al-Qaeda and its associates to retake Tal Afar was an example of something we saw elsewhere in Iraq. We recognized the problem, and we changed our strategy. Instead of coming in and removing the terrorists, and then moving on, the Iraqi government and the coalition adopted a new approach called clear, hold, and build. This new approach was made possible because of the significant gains made in training large numbers of highly capable Iraqi security forces. Under this new approach, Iraqi and coalition forces would clear a city of the terrorists, leave well-trained Iraqi units behind to hold the city, and work with local leaders to build the economic and political infrastructure Iraqis need to live in freedom.

One of the first tests of this new approach was Tal Afar. In May 2005, Colonel McMaster's unit was given responsibility for the western part of Nineveh Province where Tal Afar is located, and two months later Iraq's national government announced that a major offensive to clear the city of the terrorists and insurgents would soon be launched. Iraqi and coalition forces first met with tribal leaders and local residents to listen to their grievances. One of the biggest complaints was the police force, which rarely ventured out of its headquarters. When it did venture, it was mostly to carry out sectarian reprisals. And so the national government sent out new leaders to head the force. The new leaders set about getting rid of the bad elements, and building a professional police force that all sides could have confidence in. We recognized it was important to listen to the representatives of Tal Afar's many ethnic and religious groups. It's an important part of helping to remove one of the leading sources of mistrust.

Next, Iraqi and army coalition forces spent weeks preparing for what they knew would be a tough military offensive. They built an 8-foot high, 12-mile long dirt wall that ringed the city. This wall was designed to cut off any escape for terrorists trying to evade security checkpoints. Iraqi and coalition forces also built temporary housing outside the city, so that Tal Afar's people would have places to go when the fighting started. Before the assault on the city, Iraqi and coalition forces initiated a series of operations in surrounding towns to eliminate safe havens and make it harder for fleeing terrorists to hide. These steps took time, but as life returned to these outlying towns, these operations helped persuade the population of Tal Afar that Iraqi and coalition forces were on their side against a common enemy: the extremists who had taken control of their city and their lives.

Only after all these steps did Iraqi and coalition authorities launch Operation Restoring Rights to clear the city of the terrorists. Iraqi forces took the lead. The primary force was 10 Iraqi battalions, backed by three coalition battalions. Many Iraqi units conducted their own anti-terrorist operations and controlled their own battle space, hunting for the enemy fighters and securing neighborhoods block by block. Throughout the operation, Iraqi and coalition forces were careful to hold their fire to let civilians pass safely out of the city. By focusing on securing the safety of Tal Afar's population, the Iraqi and coalition forces begin to win the trust of the city's residents -- which is critical to defeating the *terrorists who were hiding among them.*

After about two weeks of intense activity, coalition and Iraqi forces had killed about 150 terrorists and captured 850 more. The operation uncovered weapons caches loaded with small arms ammunition and ski masks, RPG rockets, grenade and machine gun ammunition, and fuses and batteries for making IEDs. In one cache we found an ax inscribed with the names of the victims the terrorists had beheaded. And the operation accomplished all this while protecting innocent civilians and inflicting minimal damage on the city.

After the main combat operations were over, Iraqi forces moved in to hold the city. Iraq's government deployed more than a thousand Iraqi army soldiers and emergency police to keep order, and they were supported by a newly-restored police force that would eventually grow to about 1,700 officers. As part of the new strategy we embedded coalition forces with the Iraqi police and with the army units patrolling Tal Afar to work with their Iraqi counterparts and to help them become more capable and more professional. In the weeks and months that followed, the Iraqi police built stations throughout Tal Afar--and city residents began stepping forward to offer testimony against captured terrorists, and inform soldiers about where the remaining terrorists were hiding.

Inside the old Ottoman fortress, a Joint Coordination Center manned by Iraqi army and Iraqi police and coalition forces answer the many phone calls that now come into a new tip line. As a result of the tips, when someone tries to plant an IED in Tal Afar, it's often reported and disabled before it can do any harm. The Iraqi forces patrolling the cities are effective because they know the people, they know the language and they know the culture. And by turning control of these cities over to capable Iraqi troops and police, we give Iraqis confidence that they can determine their own destiny-- and that frees up coalition forces to hunt the high-value targets like Zarqawi.

The recent elections show us how Iraqis respond when they know they're safe. Tal Afar is the largest city in Western Nineveh Province. In the elections held in January 2005, of about 190,000 registered voters, only 32,000 people went to the polls. Only Fallujah had a lower participation rate. By the time of the October referendum on the constitution and the December elections, Iraqi and coalition forces had secured Tal Afar and surrounding areas. The number of registered voters rose to about 204,000 -- and more than 175,000 turned out to vote in each election, more than 85 percent of the eligible voters in Western Nineveh Province. These citizens turned out because they were determined to have a say in their nation's future, and they cast their ballots at polling stations that were guarded and secured by fellow Iraqis.

The confidence that has been restored to the people of Tal Afar is crucial to their efforts to rebuild their city. Immediately following the military operations, we helped the Iraqis set up humanitarian relief for the civilian population. We also set up a fund to reimburse innocent Iraqi families for damage done to their homes and businesses in the fight against the terrorists. The Iraqi government pledged $50 million to help reconstruct Tal Afar by paving roads, and rebuilding hospitals and schools, and by improving infrastructure from the electric grid to sewer and water systems. With their city now more secure, the people of Tal Afar are beginning to rebuild a better future for themselves and their children.

See, if you're a resident of Tal Afar today, this is what you're going to see: You see that the terrorist who once exercised brutal control over every aspect of your city has been killed or captured, or driven out, or put on the run. You see your children going to school and playing safely in the streets. You see the electricity and water service restored throughout the city. You see a police force that better reflects the ethnic and religious diversity of the communities they patrol. You see markets opening, and you hear the sound of construction equipment as buildings go up and homes are remade. In short, you see a city that is coming back to life.

The strategy that worked so well in Tal Afar did not emerge overnight -- it came only after much trial and error. It

17

took time to understand and adjust to the brutality of the enemy in Iraq. Yet the strategy is working. And we know it's working because the people of Tal Afar are showing their gratitude for the good work that Americans have given on their behalf. A recent television report followed a guy named Captain Jesse Sellars on patrol, and described him as a "pied piper" with crowds of Iraqi children happily chanting his name as he greets locals with the words "Salaam alaikum," which mean "peace be with you."

When the newswoman asks the local merchant what would have happened a few months earlier if he'd been seen talking with an American, his answer was clear: "They'd have cut off my head, they would have beheaded me." Like thousands of others in Tal Afar, this man knows the true meaning of liberation.

[T]he progress we and the Iraqi people are making is also real. And those in a position to know best are the Iraqis, themselves.

One of the most eloquent is the Mayor of Tal Afar, a courageous Iraqi man named Najim. Mayor Najim arrived in the city in the midst of the al-Qaeda occupation, and he knows exactly what our troops have helped accomplish. He calls our men and women in uniform "lion-hearts," and in a letter to the troopers of the Third Armored Cavalry Regiment, he spoke of a friendship sealed in blood and sacrifice. As Mayor Najim had this to say to the families of our fallen: "To the families of those who have given their holy blood for our land, we all bow to you in reverence and to the souls of your loved ones. Their sacrifice was not in vain. They are not dead, but alive, and their souls [are] hovering around us every second of every minute. They will not be forgotten for giving their precious lives. They have sacrificed that which is most valuable. We see them in the smile of every child, and in every flower growing in this land. Let America, their families, and the world be proud of their sacrifice for humanity and life." America is proud of that sacrifice, and we're proud to have allies like Mayor Najim on our side in the fight for freedom.

In 2005, Brigadier General Ahmed, chief of Nineveh's

provincial police, named Najim the chief of police in Tal Afar. After a short time working together, LTC Christopher Hickey, 3rd Armored Cavalry Regiment, encouraged him to take the place of the city's mayor, whose links to al-Qaeda and the insurgents who controlled Tal Afar were an open secret. Despite his not meeting the criterion of being a resident of Tal Afar, the town's leaders unanimously decided to appoint him mayor as well as police chief of the tumultuous city.

With the strong counsel, collaboration, and support of LTC Hickey and the 3rd ACR, Najim was able to quickly clear the city and to begin rebuilding its infrastructure.

I   The American Invasion and Suicide Pilots

"From the moment we confirmed that Americans had entered Iraqi airspace, we knew we were defeated."

I was an Iraqi Air Defense intelligence officer, a major, assigned to al-Qadisiyah Airbase in the predominantly Sunni al-Anbar Province of western Iraq, when American planes entered Iraqi airspace.

Al-Qadisiyah, which would soon be known as al-Asad Airbase, the second largest U.S. military airbase in Iraq, was home to three fighter squadrons of the Iraqi Air Force, operating MiG 21s and MiG 29s. It also housed a three-square-kilometer weapon-storage area.

Iraq's military was exhausted from eight years (1980-1988) of war with Iran, and weakened by U.N. sanctions that seriously hurt our technology and limited our defenses as a result of our invasion of Kuwait in 1990. Because of sanctions, we were prohibited from buying weapons and equipment. Instead, we were forced to develop, maintain, and repair what we had.

The only relatively effective technology we developed was a decoy signal that mimicked a missile signature to draw U.S. jets' fire, wasting American ammunition and creating confusion, but it was more an irritant than an effective countermeasure.

The Iraqi Air Force knew that we did not have the equipment to counter American planes and weapons if it were to come to that, so they trained about 40 pilots whose mission would be to attack coalition aircraft carriers to destroy American aircraft before they could take flight. Although it was generally unspoken, we knew that these pilots would not survive attacking the carriers.

As it turned out, they never had the chance. American bombers precluded any opportunity to use them by destroying all of our military runways and grounding our aircraft in the earliest hours of the brief war.

Craig Lancto

~~~~

Before 1990, Iraqi Air Defense was under the command of the Iraqi Air Force, and old prejudices and favoritism lingered. The Iraqi Air Force commander was a pilot who believed that war would be in the air, so he allocated little or nothing to Air Defense for firing at aircraft from the ground.

Air Defense had to make do with what it had. We had some Russian Surface-to-Air missiles (SAMs), which had good range, but the Air Force commander considered them too expensive, so when Air Defense requisitioned additional SAMs, the request was denied and the Air Force instead used the funds to purchase additional MiG 29s.We always knew that the United States forces were far too powerful for us to prevail over them in war, but we never really anticipated that they would invade. We never expected them to bring the war to Iraq.

Our military was prepared for war with Iran or Israel, but we did not expect an attack by Coalition Forces—a multinational force comprising Australia, Poland, the United Kingdom, and the United States—and we had developed no plans to mobilize our forces in the event. Air Defense was armed with vintage 1961-1962 SAMs, and a limited supply of SAM 7 shoulder-fired missiles with a 2,000-meter (about 1¼ miles) range, 57-millimeter antitank guns, and 37- and 23-mm anti-aircraft guns. Before the American jets began their attack, a battalion of SAM 6 missiles were moved to al Basra near the border with Kuwait. The SAMs were not designed for mobility. They required a full day to re-position the stations, launchers, and radar, rendering them ineffective against American planes.

The American jets entering Iraqi airspace just before 3:00 a.m. on January 17, 1991, took the Iraqi military completely by surprise.

I was sleeping in the operations center at al-Qadissiyah Airbase. The operations center was an above-ground prefab building with eight rooms and a conference room that served as our main center of operations. I was awakened by a siren sounding an incursion, but we heard the sirens often, and usually they were false alarms from a plane that had strayed over the border.

By the time I got to the operations room, though, headquarters had confirmed that American planes had penetrated Iraqi airspace.

Other than the sounds from our equipment and necessary voice

21

communications, the operations center was silent. I asked the base commander, "What will we do?"

He said. "They won't attack us."

At first we thought that the United States and Saudi Arabia might simply try to cut off the south of Iraq from Baghdad, but we never considered a full-on assault.

As soon as it was confirmed that American fighter jets had entered Iraqi airspace, we knew that we didn't stand a chance. We accepted our fate; If today was the day, then so be it.

Our commander had not made any plans for an invasion. We quickly began to make emergency and contingency plans for an attack we had never expected to come. I told the commander that we should send away our soldiers. They could do nothing against the American jets. They could do nothing here but die; keeping them at the base unnecessarily endangered their lives. Even we could do nothing but watch.

Our operations center stood a few meters from a reinforced underground bunker. With 25-30 minutes to prepare, we were ordered to a command post in one of the shelters on the airfield. We—five officers, including the base commander and his deputy, and a half-dozen soldiers, each in his own thoughts—watched the radar and readouts in silence. We listened to the incoming reports and watched the coordinates showing countless jets coming toward us, moving closer and closer. For 30-45 minutes we watched helplessly in silence, before the attack on our air base began.

From the time the first huge explosions shook our operations center, time seemed to move in slow motion, and the bombing seemed to go on forever. Other than commands to our gunners, the sound of the bombs shaking the room we stood in was the only sound we heard,

We understood immediately that this incursion was the beginning of war with the United States. We also knew that the Americans had more and better technology, and we knew that we couldn't last long. Before the first bombs fell, from the moment we confirmed that Americans had entered Iraqi airspace, we knew we were defeated.

All through that first night, we heard bombs exploding. When the bombing finally stopped, I told Major General Ali, the commanding general, "This is insanity! You have to give the order to go underground." We were all gathered in the huge shelter, Air Force and Air Defense, both. Each building at al-Asad had a hardened bunker close by, designed to withstand everything up to a direct hit from a nuclear bomb.

Finally, he gave the order. We started with the communications systems, weapons, and radar screens, and gradually moved everything from the prefab ops center to the reinforced bunker about 15 meters away. With our entire operation moved to an underground bunker, we settled in to work in 4-5 hour shifts. On the second day, the commander ordered that only officers on shift could be in the bunker. Other shifts had to find shelter elsewhere because the bunker was too crowded.

MG Ali told us to join his officers in a larger shelter. It too was hardened and better equipped than what we had put together under fire, but during the first night of bombing, we moved to smaller shelter. He took us—Air Defense—with him because we had been monitoring the situation from about two km—a little more than a mile—away.

Every officer controlled one squad or unit, and each decided independently what his unit would do. Reports from 1st Division headquarters in Baghdad came in continually. We watched the radar screens and gave our orders as the bombs rained down around us.

Early on, the base commander ordered one MiG 29 into the air to attack and send the message that Iraq's Air Force presented at least some degree of threat, but we had no contact with him and we had no idea where he was or what he was doing. While he was in the air, the Americans attacked the base. When he returned, the runway was destroyed, and I don't know how or where he landed.

On the first day of the attack, dozens of jets attacked the air base. We later learned that Americans attacked all the airbases in Iraq that day, concentrating on runways and aircraft. It was God's mercy that they did not attack buildings on the first day; they only bombed the runways, and so spared many lives. But, many of the bombs were on a delay, timed to explode even when the planes were no longer going over.

Fortunately, the bombers concentrated only on runways, not on destroying buildings or personnel. The first wave of bombs was intended to make the runways unusable so that our planes couldn't take off. They were also jamming our communications signals and their scatter bombs destroyed the runways to the extent that we couldn't even drive a car on them.

I suggested that we move to nearby caves, where we could monitor the air attacks without being in the bull's eye. The commander said no; we stay on base and the soldiers stay with us. The bunker provides shelter from the bombs, he said.

I said, "But this is where the Americans expect us to be. They are not Iranians." But my arguments fell on deaf ears.

It was terrifying. The majority of the personnel in the command post were shocked. They did their jobs, but they were stunned. From the command post we could see a big plane—maybe a Boeing 707—that we had captured when we invaded Kuwait in 1990. It was very close and as I looked out, I saw it disintegrate.

Although it was quiet throughout the hours of daylight, it was as if we all held our breath waiting for the next wave. It came with the darkness.

When night fell, the American bombers returned and completed the destruction of our runways. They also leveled the operations room we had occupied during the first attack. It was impossible not to notice that the Americans had planned the attacks for maximum damage to our defenses and minimum human casualties.

When we went outside, we saw destruction all around the bunker. We were surrounded by mines, bombs that would explode on contact, so we used flashlights and linked arms, carefully picking our way through them in the darkness.

The next wave of attacks came at around noon the following day, before all of the timed bombs had yet exploded. This attack destroyed our planes and weapons.

We continued to pressure the commander to send our soldiers away from the base for their own safety. They were of no use and their lives were in danger. He continued to refuse.

Night after night, the Americans returned to batter the base with their bombs and missiles. They destroyed many of the shelters and killed many of our engineers.

By the second and third days it was clear that the Americans were tracking radio signals from the command post, and they started attacking the bunkers. We placed the antenna 200-300 meters away near the above-ground center so that it wouldn't give away our position when we moved to the bunker, and the Americans bombed it out of existence.

We set up a second, smaller, control room 300-400 meters away, and from time to time, we changed its location. We didn't use radios at all when the American airplanes were approaching because they could home in on the signals. We had lost electricity and it was very dark. It was a very dark time.

There was one officer, Colonel Mohammed Mansour, who was a very good and brave man from Ramadi. He later commanded al Huria Air Base in Kirkuk before Saddam had him executed. As the airplanes attacked, Colonel Mohammed stood outside, where he calmly smoked cigarettes while he watched the destruction all around him.

There were now about 15 officers together in the big bunker, but we had lost all communications capacity, so MG Ali relied on wireless radios to get news from the BBC and VOA.

We had a small group of soldiers with shoulder-fired Russian Strela anti-aircraft missiles. SAM 7s were deployed around the airbase—We had 57- and 37-mm guns at Haditha Dam, about 25 miles away—but the jets remained on the ground. We were ordered to fire at the American planes, but we knew that they were way out of range, and their jamming signals threw off our radar.

Air attacks came from varying altitudes. In the beginning, low level attacks cost the U.S. some jets, so they shifted to mid- and high-altitude attacks to avoid the anti-aircraft guns around their targets.

The base commander ordered soldiers to man the artillery and anti-aircraft guns, even though he knew that the old weapons didn't have the range to reach the bombers.

Two soldiers were injured in the second attack, one of them gravely. The Air Defense commander had sent the pilots and troops under his command to safety, and again, I told the base commander that we had to send the rest of our soldiers to a safe place. "If anyone is killed here, it will be your fault for keeping them in danger even though you know they can't do anything." Finally, he ordered them to housing about 1.5 km away, a little less than a mile.

The Iran-Iraq war was a long, bloody, violent war, but compared with this America engagement....If America had happened before Iran-Iraq we would have thought Iran-Iraq was a salad. We couldn't imagine. During the Iran-Iraq war, for example, we covered our artillery in bad weather because we knew the Iranians wouldn't fly. The Americans came in all conditions, in the rain, at night...nothing stopped them.

We never expected this invasion; we had no idea what to expect, how events would play out. This was the first time for us to fight against the United States. Through eight years of fighting Iran, we thought that we had seen the worst. During the long Iran-Iraq war we said "If I get out of this alive, I will never die." How much worse could war with the vastly superior coalition forces be?

We quickly learned. When we saw the destruction from the American bombings, we knew that this was the war to get out of alive.

One night when we were alerted that the American jets were approaching, we sent soldiers to alert the officers and men who were off shift. One of the young staff officers, a lieutenant in charge of communications, was a very sound sleeper. All the officers except the lieutenant reported for duty. I asked the soldier where he was. He said, "I kept pounding on the door, shouting, 'Lieutenant, wake up! Wake up, Lieutenant!' He didn't answer, what could I do?"

After the bombs started going off all around and very close to us, the lieutenant showed up. He looked stunned: his eyes bulged, and he went for an entire day without speaking. After that he was easier to wake up.

On the third day of bombing, the Americans targeted a building that sheltered two MiG 25s, destroying the fighter jets and the officers who were with them, even though Air Defense had warned them not to stay with the jets.

In the first three days of the United States' attack in January 1991, American forces jets and cruise missiles attacked and destroyed:

1. Headquarters and Air Force and Air Defense radars
2. Communications and communications cables/junctions throughout Iraq.

3.   Military airbases
4.   Military factories and industry throughout Iraq
5.   Electric power stations
6.   Gas and oil refineries
7.   Main roads/highways
8.   Bridges
9.   Air defense units/missile brigades/squadrons/radar and observers
10. Political headquarters
11. Saddam's residences
12. Some civilian buildings
13. 200+ civilians in shelters being used as operations headquarters

The coalition used cruise missiles, British Tornadoes, French Mirage 2000s F-15s, 16s , 101s, 111s, 118s, F4E Phantoms, and F-117 stealth fighters, which we called "ghosts." They used conventional bombs, laser-guided bombs, anti-personnel bombs, missiles that lock onto radar signals, and bombs with large payloads.

Although we were ordered not to send our airships to fight, Mirage F1s from the 1st Division destroyed four; Mirages from the 2d Air Defense Division destroyed one.

Before bombing, the Americans usually set off flares to illuminate the area for visual observation and verification of targets. We told a sergeant to shoot the flares down to deny the Americans their light, but he said no. The flares are inexpensive, but the missiles are expensive.

During training, instructors had pounded on how expensive the missiles were and the importance of using them sparingly. Clearly the sergeant had learned the lesson well and would not budge on wasting missiles that cost thousands on flares that cost a few dollars—no matter what the cost in life and strategic targets.

Later, as mayor of Tal Afar, I remembered the sense of helplessness and the continual and massive destruction, and it was a large factor in my determination that airstrikes would never be used there.

When the bombing started the Minister of Education called to say that artillery shells were landing on his ministry.... Our own artillery shells, because of the 'improvements" that we had made to extend their flight.

After about three weeks at the ruined air base, I was ordered to leave the destroyed air base for Samarra.

2   An Appointment in Samarra

"The bodies of dead soldiers littered the ground; starving dogs roamed among them, eating their carcasses."

When a country is under attack, its people normally band together, as they do in any crisis. It is natural to come together for mutual protection. War is one of the worst crises we ever face; in war, we all know that each day could be our last. Of course that is true anywhere, but in war it is almost a physical presence.

Iraqi civilians were frustrated. While we were at war—during the long war with Iran, when we invaded Kuwait—they were behind us. They supported us and gave us moral support.

But now, in the north of Iraq, the Kurds told the Iraqi military to leave, and in the south the civilians took much stronger action, even firing on their own soldiers, Iraqi troops returning from Kuwait, staggering along the roads, exhausted and starving.

When I entered the military, I understood that I had a good chance of being killed. Surviving the eight-year war with Iran strengthened our belief that God had granted us extra time. We saw the dead face-to-face, but we survived.

God reminds us that surviving one day is no guarantee of seeing the end of the next. The Prophet (PBUH) told us, "Live life as if it will never end, and prepare for the afterlife as if you will die tomorrow."

Death is everywhere, even, maybe especially, when you think you are safe.

When the war with Iran ended, some units that had been on the front line had suffered many fatalities. Survivors fell back, greatly relieved that they would live to see their families again. Returning, as they pounded stakes into the ground to pitch their tents, some were killed when they hit an unexploded British bomb from World War II.

On the other hand, when an RPG (rocket-propelled grenade) hit one of our soldiers in the chest, he was critically injured, but it didn't explode. Surgeons were afraid to attempt to extract it lest it explode during the procedure. Finally, one surgeon volunteered and successfully and safely removed the grenade. These are the vagaries of war.

~~~~

Within the first 10-14 days of the American invasion, we learned that an American F-14 had been brought down about 25 miles north of al-Qadissiyah. The plane had blown up a gasoline supply depot and the resulting explosion killed and injured civilians in the area. One of the pilots was rescued by a military helicopter, but Iraqi civilians captured the other one. As Saddam had offered a big reward for American pilots, they turned him over to the Ba'athists in Baghdad for the reward.

Meanwhile, Bedouins found six or seven British SAS troops (Special Air Service, a British special forces unit that undertakes reconnaissance, counter-terrorism, direct action, hostage rescue and intelligence gathering) who had died from exposure in the desert, where it gets very cold at night, maybe -20, -25 degrees centigrade (-5, -13 degrees Fahrenheit).

After about three weeks, at the battered al-Qadissiyah Air Base, I was ordered to report to Samarra, which was surrounded by many factories run by the Ministry of Industry. These factories produced weapons and ammunition, but Americans thought they were making chemical weapons. They weren't.

When we arrived in Samarra, about 124 km (78 miles) north of Baghdad, we found the factories destroyed. Everything was destroyed, so we stayed in the desert until we found abandoned trailers next to a refinery where we could stay.

We were out of food and sent patrols out to scrounge what they could to keep up our energy. They found water and some emergency rations our troops had abandoned. Sometimes we sent soldiers to the city to find food—or flour. We had relied on army stores, and they were used up, and there was no army to rely on, no army stores. Making it much harder, we were in a stressful situation without cigarettes. Everyone smoked cigarettes.

Five or six days later, I was ordered to al Basra with a brigade. As our convoy made its way over the more than 650 km (409 miles) to Basra, we found that the bridges had been destroyed. It was slow going. Samarra was in ruin, but the devastation in Basra made Samarra look comparatively untouched. The bodies of dead soldiers littered the ground. Starving dogs roamed among them, eating their carcasses.

The coalition had specifically targeted al Basra for destruction because it is Iraq's main port and its proximity to Kuwait had established it as a staging area for invasion of that country. Az Zubair (or Az Zubayr), was a city just south of Basra until 2008, when urban sprawl merged them into one large metropolis. Greater Basra is Iraq's largest majority-Shi'a city, and it was the site of the beginning of the Shi'a revolution in 1991.

The Shatt al-Arab river in southeast Iraq flows from the confluence of the Tigris and the Euphrates to the Arab (Persian) Gulf. As it has been for more than 3,500 years, the region is interlaced with irrigation canals, although since Turkey diverted so much of the water with the construction of the Ataturk Dam, the flow has been considerably reduced.

The U.S. Air Force had destroyed the bridges on the canal from Basra-Zubair to the Arabian Gulf, so the Iraqi Army built earthen bridges over conduits that allowed the water to flow through—which the Americans destroyed almost as soon as they were completed. Crossing the canal had become so perilous that soldiers trying to reach anti-aircraft guns on the other side recited the shahada: "There is no God but God (Allah) and Mohammed is his prophet," to prepare for death before crossing.

Of course, our invasion of Kuwait had provoked the U.S. invasion. Ironically, Iraqis generally opposed invading Kuwait. Neither the Iraqi people nor the Iraqi military approved of the invasion, not that we knew about it in advance. It was sprung on us suddenly, without warning; no one wanted it, and I was not the only officer who had a bad feeling about it.

Saddam had kept his plans secret, even from the invading troops. Well, when I say "plans"...there was no real plan, no strategy, and he used the Republican Guard, the troops usually charged with protecting the president, for the invasion. It seemed impulsive. Even the Minister of Defense didn't know about it in advance. Helicopter pilots learned about their mission at the last moment. They were ordered into Kuwait with no preparation, and helicopters were crashing because they were tangled on power lines and cables. The invasion was childish—petulant.

When Saddam began massing troops on the border, we all assumed that it was saber-rattling, an intimidation tactic, but still it caused a general sense of impending disaster. When the actual invasion began, even the Iraqi troops along the border were taken by surprise.

On August 2, 1990, Iraq invaded Kuwait over several issues, the most serious were that Saddam accused the Emirate of slant-drilling, that is drilling into Iraq on an angle to steal Iraqi oil, and that Kuwait was pushing Iraq to repay more than $14 billion it had borrowed from Kuwait to finance the war against Iran. Saddam also believed—or at least claimed—that Kuwait was flooding the oil market and suppressing the price of oil, denying Iraq money that we badly needed.

The battle was over in about two days of intense fighting in which Iraq defeated or drove Kuwait's troops into Bahrain and Saudi Arabia. Almost immediately, Saddam claimed—or he would probably have said *reclaimed*— Kuwait as an Iraqi province. During the seven months that we occupied the Emirate, Iraqis set more than 600 oil wells on fire, the smoke from which continued to hover over Kuwait and southern Iraq.

Before the invasion, Saddam was popular in Kuwait. They saw him holding the line against Iran, protecting Kuwait, as well as Iraq. Iran had tried to assassinate Kuwait's prince, and on one day of the Iran-Iraq war designated "Kuwait's Revenge," Iraq fired more than 100 missiles at Iran along with incursions by Iraqi aircraft. I believe that Kuwaitis liked him more than they liked their own prince.

Invading Kuwait was stupid, but Iraq owed $14 billion to Kuwait for money we had borrowed to finance our eight-year war against Iran, and Kuwait's government was making increasingly insistent demands for payment. Saddam could have appealed directly to the Kuwaiti people and they would have helped him, but instead….

Kuwait, Saudi Arabia, and Iraq engaged in discussions about the debt. Saddam was panicking. He accused Kuwait and the United Arab Emirates of exceeding oil production quotas to lower oil prices and damage Iraq's economy.

As is true throughout the Middle East, modern day problems are the continuation of instability and strife that has a history that stretches back thousands of years, and they do not exist in a vacuum. More than in other parts of the world our long, complicated history and shifting borders were an unspoken (usually) party to discussions and negotiations.

~~~~~~

A snapshot of Iraq's recent history

Iraq has a history of violence. Consider, for example, the fate of two kings who were deposed as recently as the 1950s

After World War I, the British administered Iraq as the "British Mandate of Mesopotamia" until 1933, when it became the independent Kingdom of Iraq. The British installed the Hashemite (i.e., descendants of Hashim ibn 'Abd Manaf, the Prophet's great grandfather) King Faisal I after the French ejected him from Syria, where he had ruled as King of the Arab Kingdom of Syria in 1920. He ruled as King of Iraq from August 1921 to 1933. Iraq became a republic after a coup d'état in 1958.

Around 1950, Iraq had an excellent relationship with Great Britain. The British thought that Iraq and Jordan should unite. Both kings were of the Hashemite dynasty.

The prime minister said that Iraq barely had the resources to support its own people and Jordan was very poor, but, he suggested, if the British would return Kuwait, which they had created out of Iraq's Basra Willayet in 1921, the three countries together could support each other.

The British countered with a proposal to give the Arabistan region of Iran, adjoining Basra, to Iraq.

In 1952, Egyptians revolted against their king, Farouk, for his lavish lifestyle, incompetent governance, and corrupt government. They deposed him but they let him live. When he fled to Monaco, he left as a national hero. Senior officers bade him farewell and honored him with a 21-gun salute. The 300-pound exiled king died at table in a restaurant in Rome, following a characteristically large meal. He was 45 years old.

In 1958, the Iraqi army revolted against their young

Hashemite king, Faisal, cousin to King Hussein of Jordan. When the soldiers were ordered to Jordan to assist King Hussein, they marched instead on the palace in Baghdad where the king surrendered peacefully, his Qur'an in hand. The soldiers ordered him, Crown Prince Abdullah, Abdullah's wife and mother, Faisal's aunt, and several servants to the courtyard, where they were told to face the wall before the soldiers cut them down with machine guns. Only Abdullah's wife survived. The prime minister was killed the next day. King Faisal was 23 years old.

In 2003, when the regime fell, I didn't see any poor people stealing and looting. It was wealthy men who took advantage of the chaos to increase their fortune.

Maybe it is the extremes in weather that makes so many Iraqis unpredictable. The weather goes from extreme summer heat to extreme winter cold with no fall and no spring between.

3   The al-Basra Uprising

*"The insurgents were vicious, inhuman, committing such atrocities as
forcing captives to drink Benzene and then shooting them with
hollow-point bullets to set them aflame."*

We returned to Basra in three cars, the only cars heading south;
all the other traffic was moving north. We could see the thick cloud
of smoke still hovering over Kuwaiti oil fields.

Along the route we saw groups of soldiers, hungry and tired,
plodding the nearly 300 miles from Basra to Baghdad, some eating
grass to survive, some sick from eating grass to survive, and still
others who lay where they had died along the road, dogs eating their
decaying flesh. When troops passing us in the opposite direction
asked where we were going, we said "Basra." They urged us to go
back, saying, "There is no Basra."

We arrived in Basra on the day of the cease-fire, almost exactly
100 hours after the war started. As I said earlier, communications
systems had been destroyed and families had no way to hear from
their loved ones who had been caught up in the war. My wife,
Zahara, was in Mosul caring for our two young children and in the
eighth month of pregnancy with our third, when a soldier went to our
home to tell her that I was dead.

"I cried and cried," Zahara said, "and I lost the baby girl I was
carrying. His mother and I both believed that he was dead. The
soldier who came said that he was the last to get out of Basra alive."

Food, already scarce, was becoming more so. There was no traffic
moving, so we received no supplies for four days after the
Americans stopped bombing. The commander sent me with three or
four soldiers to return to Samarra to scrounge cable for
communications.

We drove the 400-plus miles north back to Samarra and then
returned to Basra with all the cable we could find. When I went to
Samarra for supplies my unit returned to the school where we were
staying in a suburb of Basra. We used a school in a civilian

neighborhood as our headquarters because the Americans were targeting military sites. We had a number of contingencies planned as our military bases were steadily being destroyed.

That same day, American tanks, artillery and ground troops under the command of Colonel Herbert R. McMaster entered Iraq. Colonel McMaster, now retired lieutenant general and former national security advisor, would play a much larger role in Iraq's destiny—and mine.

~~~~

Throngs of exhausted Iraqi troops returning from Kuwait crowded a wooden bridge that replaced one bombed out by the Americans across the Satalarb River. Traveling in the opposite direction, we didn't see how we could cross against that tidal wave of soldiers, so eight of us, three officers and five soldiers commandeered a rowboat to cross the river to meet MG Sadi Zhazem, the Army chief of staff.

An exhausted Sadi told us that the invasion of Kuwait had been a disaster. We had taken huge casualties, a terrible loss of soldiers and great destruction of tanks and equipment.

"You can imagine judgment day," he said, "but you can't imagine what happened there—the disturbing things we saw."

We saw the troops, exhausted, starving, discouraged, and dying. We saw the dead left where they fell. We went on.

We didn't know what to expect from the American forces. We didn't know whether they were going to invade the city. We had no idea what they were doing. Our communications were cut off. We had only a small radio and our information came from Kuwaiti radio. The radio station from Baghdad was out; we couldn't get Voice of America or BBC. The Kuwaiti station reported that Iraq was in full revolution with fighting in the streets.

We couldn't go to Kuwait. Before Saddam invaded, we had excellent relations; after we invaded, not so good. Saddam had envisioned a reunion of Iraq and Kuwait. He sent an emissary to negotiate with Saudi Arabia and Kuwait, but I think that he sent the wrong man. He said that Kuwait had joined with the United States to destroy Iraq's economy with high oil prices.

We heard contradictory rumors. The media speculated that the United States had urged Saddam to invade Kuwait. We heard that Saudi Arabia had approved of Saddam's plan to invade Kuwait.

The Saddam regime was harsh and unforgiving. We had no one we could talk to for an honest situation report. We didn't know whom we could trust. We didn't dare express doubts.

Of course, Saddam didn't trust anyone. Neither the minister of defense nor the army chief of staff knew about the invasion until they heard about it on the radio. Who would imagine that we would invade such a close ally?

I called General Ahmed, a close friend who had been with me at al-Assad (and later would be chief of Nineveh's police force), and we talked honestly.

Saddam had killed Ahmed's cousin, Sultan al-Jubouri, a captain in the Republican Guard who had been part of a plot to kill Saddam. The captain had spoken against Saddam to Ahmed and me, but generally people were afraid to talk.

I knew very well that the Iraqi people did not like our invasion of Kuwait. Among their intimates, they ridiculed the invasion and made fun of Saddam.

~~~~

There was an old woman who lived in the town my family comes from. Her son brought some equipment back from Kuwait after the invasion. His mother stood in front of her door and forbade him to bring anything from Kuwait into her house. It is *haram,* she said, forbidden, an offense in the sight of Allah.

Her son said, "But I bought it."

She spat on him and threw her shoe at him, two of the gravest insults in Arab culture. Her son lost his head at the insults and killed her. Of course, that meant that her family had to hunt him for revenge.

Surah 2 of the Qur'an says, "He gives wisdom to whom He wills, and whoever has been given wisdom has certainly been given much good. And none will remember except those of understanding."

I think Saddam lacked the gift of wisdom. He was impetuous and rushed important decisions.

Most Iraqis acknowledge that the people in Basra are the kindest and most generous in Iraq.

I think the so-called "Basra Uprising" in 1991 was not local people. I believe that outside agitators—especially radical clerics from Iran—were behind the uprising. I believe that not only because of the reputation that the people of Basra enjoyed as kind and generous, but also because many of the citizens came to us and said, "You are going to be attacked. If you want, we will hide you in our homes or give you civilian clothes so that you can blend in with civilians." The Iranians were still seeking revenge for the long war we fought with them. They knew that our army was weak from the long years of war with them and then Kuwait, and they wanted to take advantage of us while we were in that weakened state. I think they instigated the insurrection in al Basra.

"Uprising" doesn't usually mean killing your own soldiers, who are exhausted and starving, while they are trying to protect you.

When we reached Basra, we found that the insurgents had killed government troops and destroyed government buildings. They attacked the Ministry of Agriculture and I saw them destroy Basra's universities and the computers in every office they could access. They destroyed schools and hospitals and the office that issues identification cards. Why would the citizens of Basra do that to their own city? That is not a civil uprising; that is enemy action.

After the bombings in 1991, I was ordered to Samarra to support the single intelligence officer left there, and I had a deputy who could remain at al-Qadissiyah.

I stayed there four or five days until the Americans destroyed what was left of our base in Samarra. Then our unit—maybe 12-15 officers and 100 or so enlisted—was sent to Basra. Some squadrons were reassigned to Sheabba Airbase.

When we reached the airbase at Basra at about 2 a.m., we were exhausted. Temporary headquarters had been set up in a public school. The commander, Brigadier General Khalid, told us that his troops had been there for three or four days, and without offering any reason, he warned that we should go to Zubayr—about 18 km (11 miles) south—immediately. He seemed very anxious and remained vague about the reason, saying only that he needed to find a proper army base with provisions.

One of our officers said that we could scrounge food and necessities, but the commander just kept repeating that they had to leave.

Despite his urgent warning, we fell quickly into a deep sleep, only to wake early the next morning to the sounds of a mob shouting anti-Saddam slogans. We had never heard such open rebellion in the streets of Iraq before. It was the very beginning of what now is called "The [Shi'a] Uprising" against Saddam.

Another schoolhouse near where we slept housed Iraqi intelligence agents, not military intelligence officers—more like the Iraqi version of the CIA. We were very worried when we saw them rush out, throw their gear in a car, and evacuate without a word.

Shortly after their hurried evacuation, a delegation of some six or seven local civilians appeared at the schoolhouse with a warning:

Agitators, most likely Iranian clerics and spies with connections to Iranian intelligence, had been inciting rebellion in the south. We were in grave danger, they said, and they urged us to exchange our uniforms for civilian clothes or go to stay with them in their homes, because our headquarters was about to be attacked.

We soon realized that the Basrans who warned us had provided good information, as we experienced small arms fire from the buildings behind the school. We were hurrying to pack our cars when we came under fire from civilians. We didn't want to engage in a firefight with them, so we left as fast as we could.

We—five or six officers and twenty or so soldiers—headed farther south to the Shaiba Airbase, where we met with the regimental commander Colonel Mijbeh, a very, very good man. We found him alone at headquarters. The rest of the regiment was gone. He said, "Many senior officers came through from Kuwait, and they ask why I stay here. It is simple. I am a soldier. I don't leave my post unless I have orders to do so. Without new orders, I remain here."

Afterwards, I realized that rumblings about an uprising had likely been the reason for the commander's hurried escape from the schoolhouse. It took two or three hours to return the short distance to Az Zubayr, usually a 20-minute trip. When we arrived, Brigadier General Khaled came to us and criticized us for not leaving when he told us to.

General Khaled asked why we didn't leave the school when he warned us.

I said, "Why didn't you explain? Why didn't you tell us that we were going to be attacked?"

But I knew why. He probably didn't tell us, not only because of his great haste to get away, or because he was afraid of losing face with us by being scared off by threats from civilians. The most compelling reason that he could not warn us of the danger was that he was afraid of Saddam. Under his regime, if he had learned that we fled....

BG Khaled's brother was the divisional commander; he might have warned his brother privately, but if his brother passed the information along, he could find himself out of favor with Saddam, and that often was not a survivable situation.

The general said that when the insurgents had confronted him, he told them that he understood their anger and frustration, but they were young and energetic, and he was too old and tired to join them. Events escalated quickly and Basra became a rebel stronghold, lost to Saddam's government in Baghdad.

Cut off from supplies and other military units, we put on civilian clothes and returned to Basra. By this time, Americans had set up checkpoints between Zubayr and Nasiriyah, a little more than a hundred miles to the northwest, near the ancient city of Ur. We were not in a good situation. We had American forces between us and Kuwait and Nasiriyah, northwest of Basra. We had nowhere to go, so we stayed.

The "uprising" lasted 15-20 days before the government reacted, and then it was an overreaction. The Special Republican Guard and intelligence service sought revenge, and they killed many civilians, innocent along with the guilty. Many innocent people.

We heard that Ali Hussan al-Majid, Saddam Hussein's cousin who was in charge of security in southern Iraq, personally had executed many of the captured rebels in Sa'ad Square.

My unit—six officers and about forty soldiers, some from Basra—was flanked and surrounded. We sent out scouts in civilian clothes for a situation report on circumstances and events in the city. I should explain that Americans might find it difficult to understand the relationship between Iraqi officers and enlisted men. We do not have the same separation between officers and enlisted that you see in the United States. We were close and it was more important than ever to maintain a good relationship so that they would bring back reliable reports and not give away our position to the rebels.

We had news that a general called Ahmed Hammash had came to Az Azubayr with a few troops. His unit was ironically called the VII Corps. It was ironic because a corps is usually two or more divisions so it was a grandiose term for 50-60 soldiers, but the American forces could have learned from General Hammash how to clear a city.

General Hammash cleared the greater Basra-Azubayr metropolitan area, the second largest city in Iraq, in only a few days. He cleared Azubayr in two. As other troops joined him, including Gen Walid and his troops from the Republican guard, he was able to clear most of Basra itself in about five.

At the beginning of the uprising, insurgents attacked the Ministry of Trade's huge store, which sold products—usually Russian products—at very low prices with ration coupons. They cleaned it out. Stole everything.

As word of the uprising spread, so did insurgency throughout the country. The insurgents were vicious, inhuman, committing such atrocities as forcing captives to drink benzene and then shooting them with hollow-point bullets to set them aflame.

First Lieutenant Naji Khairullah and I changed into civilian clothes and went to his neighborhood, al-Latif, to see how the Iraqi army had cleared the neighborhood of rebels. It was simple, logical, and efficient.

They went from neighborhood to neighborhood and gave everyone five minutes to clear out of their homes and go to containment areas, men in one and women in another. They used schools, or whatever large buildings were available.

After 30 minutes, the army began a house-to-house search for people and weapons. Anyone remaining in the house was considered an insurgent, the enemy.

In the containment areas, there were people they simply called "identifiers," neighborhood residents who generally knew who the terrorists were. The soldiers would have the people from the neighborhood sit on the floor and walk among them with the identifiers who would point out who the insurgents were. Unfortunately, this also made it possible for some identifiers to settle old scores.

After the rebels were identified, the rest of the people were allowed to return to their own neighborhoods, but not to go to any others. After four or five days, the whole city of Basra had been cleared and brought again under government control. Gradually the military units were able to move freely about the city.

We heard that some rebels were taken to Baghdad, some were questioned by Ali Hussan, better known to Westerners as Chemical Ali, who was executed in January 2010 for war crimes, crimes against humanity, and genocide. There is no need to speculate about those interrogations.

In Basra, security was fragile at the beginning but improved day by day. The army set up checkpoints on the main roads and municipal services were restored, although the electric grid, destroyed by American bombs, was out of service for several months. Repairs were further delayed by the insurgents who stole tools and equipment.

Military equipment also suffered widespread destruction and the military had to reduce their forces, redistribute weapons and equipment, and cannibalize ruined equipment to salvage what they could.

From Basra to Kuwait, the roads were littered with entire convoys destroyed by American bombs. The devastation was extensive and dramatic. Soldiers crawled over the wrecked vehicles to salvage usable parts.

Because of bad communications, my family—my wife and children were staying with my parents—did not hear from me for so long that they believed—again—that I was dead.

Slowly, life in Basra returned to normal.

I served in Basra as the intelligence officer at an antiaircraft unit for five or six months. We were short on equipment, weapons, ammunition, everything. Soldiers were gathering and redistributing weapons and undergoing retraining. Many army units had been reduced or eliminated because there was not enough equipment or arms to go around.

In August 1991 I was reassigned to the antiaircraft unit at the atomic energy plant in southern Baghdad.

Craig Lancto

4 Transitions

*"...we had meeting after meeting to prepare for the war we knew we
could not avoid and could not win. "*

The Nida Factory, WMDs, and the Osirak Atomic Energy Plant

Until 1991, U.S. reconnaissance failed to find Iraqi weapons. The
Nida factory—one of the sites the U.S. believed was manufacturing
weapons of mass destruction—was an advanced facility that
manufactured al-Hussein class missiles. It was one of the production
facilities run by the Ministry of Industry and Military Industrialization,
which was headed by Saddam's son-in-law, Hussain Kamil. In 1989,
Kamil declared that he was instituting an industrial program to
provide all of the country's defense weapon and equipment needs,
exclusively with domestic resources, by 1991.

Kamil, who also had run Iraq's Secret Service Organization,
applied covert intelligence techniques to industrial espionage to
acquire the needed technology. The versatile factory was capable of
manufacturing virtually any equipment or machines the country
needed. But no WMDs.

In August 1991 I was reassigned to the antiaircraft unit at the
Osiris-class nuclear reactor site in southern Baghdad. It was built by
the French, who called it Osirak; (sometimes Osiraq, playing on the
name of the country). Iraqis called it Tammuz 1, after the name of
the Babylonian month when the Ba'ath party—Saddam's party—
came to power in 1968. The buildings surrounding the reactor, which
included massive research buildings, about 35 meters high and four
kilometers in total length, were encased in earthworks.

It was a small plant but some radioactivity lingered in the area.
There were three reactors in the facility. In addition to the French
reactor, the site contained one Russian and one Italian reactor.
Israel destroyed the French reactor in "Operation Opera," a 1981
preemptive strike also known as "Operation Babylon," but research
facilities that surrounded it were still protected. Several Iraqis and a

43

French researcher were killed in that raid. Americans destroyed the remaining two reactors. I was assigned to the facility as intelligence officer for the Air Defense unit.

Air Defense units at Tammuz 1 were the elite of Air Defense, experienced and well-trained. Unlike many other others, Air Defense units always were maintained at full strength. Between 1991 and 2003, tensions between Iraq and the United States ran high. During that time there were two major airstrikes and many smaller ones, so when UN inspectors came, we moved everything in anticipation of American bombing that we knew would follow.

~~~

The facility remained very secure, but we mounted SAMs on the roof. When I worked there in the 1980s, we called it the first perimeter or the belt of fire. When I arrived there in 1991 I found that some of the SAMs were buried under the dirt. About 70 of the guards died in the bombings.

Only surface-to-air missiles, 57- mm batteries, remained in place, with one infantry unit to protect the plant. Although the reactor was destroyed, agricultural research continued in the compound's facilities. The facilities, now controlled by the military, were extensive, with about 3,000 personnel, including scientists and support staff. But the research was unrelated to atomic energy. For example, sugar prices were high, so the lab developed a method for extracting sugar from dates.

After the American attack, Saddam Hussein demonstrated new respect for Air Defense. The Air Force had been ineffective. In fact, jets were not a factor at all in the brief war, so in 1990, he removed Air Defense from the aegis of the Air Force.

We had 47 SAM-2 and SAM-3 batteries, called Volga and Bijora. at the nuclear site. They required a great deal of maintenance and we took spare parts from the old, obsolete batteries to keep them in operation. We had to move them every day because of the satellite- and U2 spy plane surveillance. Every battery commander had two daily options for new locations.

Nevertheless, with the destruction to the physical plant at the reactor site, the missiles were withdrawn from the area.

~~~~

Meeting Zahara

As I mentioned, in 1985 I was an intelligence officer with

Iraqi Air Defense, assigned to the nuclear facility near Baghdad. In anticipation of an all-out American attack on the facility, we had been ordered to find strategic locations for machine gun emplacements with unobstructed sight lines to the facility.

We located a school that met our requirements near the facility, and I told the principal that we were going to place machine guns on the roof of her school.

She said no. "This is a school not an army camp, and I will not permit weapons on the roof."

More than a little taken aback, I told her that the president had ordered us to place these machine guns.

She said to tell the president that we were not placing machine guns on the roof of her school.

I used every argument at my disposal, but the principal absolutely refused to budge. In the end, we had our machine gun emplacement—on an earthen mound we built near the school.

But I returned to see the principal with increasing frequency. Although we were assigned to the nuclear facility and were not supposed to leave, I would find an officer to cover for me while I took what became my daily trips to visit the principal. I wore out three car engines during the courtship of the principal who became my wife eight months later.

~~~~~~~~~~~~~~

In 1998 the United States accused Iraq of attempting to assassinate President George H.W. Bush in Kuwait. In retaliation, they bombed the Jihaz al-Mukhabarat al-Amma, Iraq's General Intelligence Directorate under Saddam Hussein.

Iraqi technology

The 1991 war and the sanctions after that war had taken a serious toll, not only on the military, but on the Iraqi people. The fabric of society had been irreparably torn; the people suffered greatly. Soldiers didn't have the money to travel from one unit to the next. We needed time to recover, but instead we faced extended friction with Israel and Palestine, and there never was time. We lacked medical care for our sick and wounded.

Out of necessity, Iraq began developing weapons on its own. We improved and extended gun barrels so ammunition that was intended to go 3 kilometers traveled farther and at greater velocity.

Some munitions were timed and we manipulated them to extend the time, which almost literally blew up in our faces in 2003, when the shells exploded so late that instead of exploding at the apogee of their arc, they went off on the ground, killing and wounding our own people.

Scientists not only improved missile fuel's velocity and distance, but they also developed a signal to simulate that of a missile battery to decoy American missiles.

To detect enemy aircraft entering Iraqi airspace, we went "old school." In addition to radar, we used redundant human observation, doubling the necessary number of men with over-sized T3K binoculars keeping watch on the borders with Kuwait, Saudi Arabia, and Iran.

Saddam gave Air Defense additional funds, but the technological gap continued to be huge. I remained at the energy plant until 1996, when I was assigned to Air Defense headquarters in Baghdad as intelligence officer. My work included SAM batteries, tracking status, condition, and so on, and I forwarded my reports to my supervisor who passed them on to Air Defense General Command.

Weapons of Mass Destruction, 2003

In 2003, I was assigned to the First Division in Baghdad as security adviser to the Air Defense Commander.

U.S. forces used Cruise missiles and long range jet fire, and we had little or nothing to answer them. Our Surface-to-Air Missiles (SAMs) were burdensome and inefficient. Because of the spy planes and satellites, we had to move them every day, and it took all day to move them. By the time they were moved, U.S. satellites had identified their new positions and we had to relocate them again. The U.S. destroyed many of them, killing many Iraqi soldiers along with them.

Another obstacle was more embarrassing and far more discouraging. We suffered a serious desertion rate, officers as well as enlisted men, sometimes entire units disappearing en masse. As I mentioned earlier, we encountered one battalion where only the commander remained. Every officer and soldier under him had vanished before the war we knew was coming.

~~~

Under Saddam, Camp Taji, Headquarters of the 1st Armored Division, about 20-25 miles north of Baghdad, was al-Taji airfield, an Iraqi Republican Guard base under the command of Major General Karim al-Felahi. It was another site believed to be a chemical-weapon manufacturing site, and when it was taken, Coalition forces found thousands of empty canisters apparently designed to be filled with chemical weaponry, but no chemical weapons.

Because the Americans knew all of our official locations, we moved our headquarters to a conference room at Baghdad University.

A month or so before the "Shock and Awe" campaign, the Ministry of Defense called about 200 senior officers, mostly brigadier and major generals, to a meeting with the Minister of Defense in Baghdad. Sultan Hashem, Minister of Defense told us that the Iraqi government had done everything it could to avoid war, to convince the Americans not to attack, but the Americans were not listening; they had made up their minds. He asked what we could do other than put up the best fight we could manage, to fight as hard as we could against them.

"War is coming," he said. "It will happen and we know very well that our military power is nothing compared to theirs. But what can we do? We are soldiers. We will fight them."

He was distraught. His face was grim. It said that he knew someone above him had made a serious error, had done something to bring us to this point. He couldn't express it in words, but his face said it.

We expected the war to last three months, maybe as much as six. Our consensus was that, at best, Iraq could hold out for about three months. I don't think anyone predicted that it would, in fact, be over in three weeks.

On February 5, 2003, we watched Colin Powell, the American Secretary of State, announce that we had weapons of mass destruction. We watched him show slides that he said showed that Saddam had mounted bio-weapons on trucks. He supported his claim by saying that they would be impossible to find. We knew we had something, maybe chemical weapons, maybe some uranium, but we did not have nuclear weapons or any weapons of mass destruction the United States claimed they knew we had.

My family lived close to the nuclear plant, where I worked—sometime called the 777 Project—in Baghdad. I told them to go to stay with my family in Mosul.

Meanwhile, we had meeting after meeting to prepare for the war we knew we could not avoid and could not win. We began stockpiling food and supplies. We prepared machine gun emplacements and missile batteries, buried mines, dug moats and gave speeches to our troops to raise morale. Preparations focused on protecting Baghdad, protecting Saddam. Baghdad was circled by defenses intended to make the city a graveyard for American ground forces. But it was all wasted effort. The Americans laid waste to it all from the air long before the first ground troops were near the city.

We knew when the Americans were coming because they always preceded a ground attack by missile- and air attacks.

We began hearing reports of an impending American attack on some of our camps. And then we heard bombing begin and we heard missiles striking. They just continued raining down, louder and longer than anything I had heard before. I thought that it would never stop.

Later, as mayor of Tal Afar, I remembered the sense of helplessness and the continual and massive destruction, and it was a major factor in my determination that airstrikes would never be used there.

When British and American troops attacked al Basra and took the area, we knew that this was not like any war we had known.

When the bombing started, the minister of education called to say that artillery shells were landing on his ministry: our own artillery shells, because of the 'improvements" that we had made to extend their flight.

48

5   Dissolution of the Iraqi Army

"I think abruptly disbanding the Iraqi Army was one of the greatest
mistakes America made in terms of Iraq's future and stability."

Dissolution of the Iraqi Army

I was a brigadier general when the regime collapsed in 2003. We had all been sent home, when Paul Bremer, presidential envoy to Iraq, discharged the military via a televised announcement. As the top civilian administrator of the former Coalition Provisional Authority in Iraq, Bremer ruled by decree. His first decree banned the ruling Ba'ath party–Saddam's party. His second decree dismantled the Iraqi Army.

We were stunned.

Bremer claimed that Iraqi leaders had urged him to do so, but I think that he and the United States at least share the responsibility. Americans always seemed to listen only to one side, and that is always a mistake.

I think that abruptly disbanding the Iraqi Army was one of the greatest mistakes America made in terms of Iraq's future and stability. It would have been better to regroup and reorganize the army to improve stability and security.

Like my brothers in arms, as a military officer I relied on my salary to support my family, and our financial support was just cut off. No pay; no pension. What were Paul Bremer and the U.S. thinking? How did they expect us to live? So all of those fighting men were set adrift with no money and nothing to keep them occupied.

What could go wrong?

People who lose their jobs for a few months typically get some support, unemployment benefits or something, but we received nothing, and Iraqi families tend to be larger than American families and the economic instability in Iraq was further shaken by this flood of suddenly unemployed soldiers. How did they think we could survive? Did they know—did they think about—how hard it is for a father to see his children suffer? Did they expect us to throw roses at them?

This is one good example of why so many Iraqis hated Americans.

But we struggled through the interim and I emerged much later, employed in a role no one wanted in a city controlled by terrorists.

Struggling through the interim

Maybe I was lucky. My wife was a teacher and earned enough— just enough—to feed our family and reduce the suffering, but not enough to eliminate it. In Iraqi culture, in Arab culture, it is very difficult for a man to stay at home while his wife is working. It is difficult to explain the shame that an Arab man feels at having to depend on a woman to support him.

At least we lived in military housing and didn't have to pay rent. I started looking for work, but there were no jobs. Circumstances forced us to accept work in jobs we never expected, or would have considered if we were not desperate...unskilled jobs, jobs we weren't prepared for, physically or mentally. Proud military officers working at jobs no one wanted.

For example, some former officers waited for days in gas lines to fill their tanks so they could resell it on the street. Some of my friends and I started buying cars and reselling them for very little profit. Those were harsh and brutal days, the likes of which we had never seen in Iraq.

Finally, a friend offered me a job as an editor with a Baghdad magazine. I was there a couple of months earning about $150 a month—and prices were rising steeply.

I had lived in this misery for about two years altogether when an old friend, a close friend, General Ahmed, who had served with me in Air Defense at al-Qadisiyah and the atomic energy plant, telephoned to ask me to meet with him in Mosul. He had become the police chief for Nineveh Province in northern Iraq.

6   Seven Days to Tal Afar

"We spent the entire night under the fire of light machine guns."

General Ahmed was very busy because Nineveh Province was a hot spot. Nineveh's entire western border adjoins Syria, offering an inviting opportunity for terrorists to cross back and forth. And they did. And they do. Then it was al -Qaeda; now it is DAESH. We used to see the chaos and disruption in Nineveh reported regularly on the news, especially in a town called Tal Afar, the hottest spot in tumultuous Nineveh.

Since the town was known to be difficult for public safety officers, some rejected the assignment outright, some chose to resign rather to accept assignment there.

After my old friend warmly greeted me we had a long talk about family, as is typical in Iraq, before he came to the reason he had asked me to meet with him.

"I want to ask you something," he said. "There is a difficult spot called Tal Afar. I'm not going to be evasive...Let me be honest with you: I have asked sixty-four police officers to go to Tal Afar to be the chief of police. All of them have refused. Some said they would resign first."

"The city is dangerous, but through my knowledge and experience with the people, I think you might succeed there. I want to enlist you and give you this position right away."

He talked almost poetically about our nation and our duty. It is a wonderful country he said, and we all must make sacrifices to heal her wounds.

"So, what do you think?"

I didn't hesitate. I said, "Okay! I will take the job."

He said, "Okay. Get yourself ready. I'll give you a week–seven days–to gather ten men you trust to be your bodyguards. I will enlist them in the police force as well, and I will provide you anything you want or need to do the job, to restore order."

So I chose ten men from the Jubouri tribe, ten trusted relatives. They were eager to go. They all had served in the military and they did not fear battle.

In preparation, I tried to learn as much as I could about Tal Afar and its people, but I couldn't find anyone who could give me a clear idea of what the people of Tal Afar are like. I knew only that it was a dangerous place and security was very bad.

Seven days later, a convoy of about 15 vehicles filled with men and equipment made its way west from Mosul, in central Nineveh, to Tal Afar. It was only about 63 kilometers—less than 40 miles—but it seemed like a hazardous expedition across a desert.

Tal Afar: Status Quo Ante and the Castle

When we reached Tal Afar, we entered without resistance and drove to the ancient Ottoman castle that housed the police department. But when we entered the castle, we saw no sign of military or police officers, only a number of civilians. The brigadier general who had led our convoy called a Colonel Ishmael, whom I later learned was the current chief of police in Tal Afar, the man I was there to replace.

In 2004, Nineveh Province was riddled with terrorist activity. al - Qaeda and their terrorist brethren controlled the police in nearly every jurisdiction other than those under Kurdish control near the autonomous region of Kurdistan.

When Colonel Ishmael arrived, the brigadier told him that the provincial police chief had named me to replace him as chief of police in Tal Afar.

I asked. "Where are the police? This is supposed to be the police station for a town of 200,000—250,000 people."

He told me that most of them were at home. He had ordered them to stay in their homes because al -Qaeda was spread throughout the city and having them stay at home distributed the police better among them. It was better for following their activities.

"So," I asked, "who is manning police headquarters?"

"We have three barracks on the roof over police headquarters with a PK machine gun and two or three others around the castle."

It was ridiculous. The policemen were all in civilian clothes. No uniforms or any indication that they were police officers, and the police worked only with their own tribes. The Shi'a lived very close to the castle, and the Sunni in a different direction. Colonel Ishmael told his officers—he said that he had about 80—to stay in their homes and to fight the insurgents along with their own tribes. He had made no move toward organization.

This was the first major problem I faced in the city: Eighty police officers in civilian clothes to maintain order in a city of more than 200,000—and they were staying in their homes!

When the convoy left Tal Afar after a couple of hours, I became aware of steady gunfire directed at the castle. It was Sunni hoping to get off a lucky shot at anyone in the castle. I asked the ten people I brought with me to stay close to me all the time. I told them that they were to stay in the castle barracks. We spent the entire first night under the fire of light machine guns.

At about 10:00 on our second morning in Tal Afar, several Bradley Troop Carriers arrived with an American lieutenant colonel called Davis. I don't think I ever knew his first name. He already knew that I was there. He sat with me and we talked about the current situation in Tal Afar. Until that day, I knew nothing about American forces in Iraq. I knew nothing about their relationship with Iraqi forces.

LTC Davis told me that Col. Ishmael (or Ismael) Faris, the police chief I replaced, was very bad, cruel, and corrupt. Davis had heard reports of prisoners in the castle being tortured. He said that Ishmael abused citizens and had bad relations with the Sunni, which caused unrest in the city.

Although it was unspoken, I came to believe that the Americans had pushed the provincial government in Nineveh to replace him. LTC Davis said that he hoped that I could change the image of police in this town.

I told him that I would sincerely do my best, but I said that I already saw many obstacles in the way; the police are completely disorganized and undisciplined.

I didn't see any sign of enthusiasm in LTC Davis. He said he wanted the situation to get better, but he didn't seem to have his heart in supporting the effort. He didn't seem especially eager to help. He was going through the motions, but there was no passion.

Two days later, LTC Davis came back and asked me to accompany him to the prison. He asked prisoners to remove their shirts and he showed me evidence of torture. Davis became very angry. He said, "We asked you to make change and you have done nothing."

I said, "Listen to me, Colonel Davis. The Qur'an says that God took six days to make the world. It will take me more than two days to make change. You expect me to correct the wrongs of my predecessor in two days? That isn't even enough time to identify all the problems."

"You came to me two days ago to complain about the previous police chief and now you come here two days later to complain about me! I am still trying to find out who is who and what is what."

"I sincerely want to improve the situation here, but don't expect me to change everything in two days."

He looked as if he accepted my answer. He seemed to believe that I was sincere about making change.

"Well," he said, "I hope you will work as quickly as you can to change the situation here."

I assigned one of the ten men I brought with me to supervise the prison to make sure that there was no further abuse. At the same time, I sat on the ground with each of the prisoners, one by one, and asked them about their treatment and what had brought them here.

Some had been arrested with lawful warrants and were detained awaiting trial. Three or four had been detained without a warrant.

I sent for the officer who arrested them and asked why they were here. He said that he had very reliable information that they are terrorists. I said, "You have two hours to find a judge and provide all the evidence and information that you have, and the judge will make a decision. If I do not see a warrant I will hold you personally responsible."

He said, "We can't reach the judge because he lives in a Sunni neighborhood and it would be too dangerous to go there." So I called my friend, the provincial chief of police and asked him to call the chief judge of Nineveh province to assign a judge to stay at the castle or to execute warrants so the police would have no excuse to detain prisoners without one.

This didn't work out as well as we thought, but after a while we worked out a system to either escort a judge to interview the detainees at the castle or to take the detainees to the judge until we had a lawful warrant for every prisoner detained.

We also found that the prisoners were being fed very poorly. We had little or no food for them or the police officers. So despite being surrounded by terrorists who were firing at us, people in the Shi'a neighborhood began providing meals for us.

The Sunnis hated the police. They had not fared well under the previous chief, and a police force that was entirely Shi'a. It's a cultural thing. Now they knew the police were there to protect them.

We worked to upgrade and supplement the simple food with whatever we could get. If we had onions, I would call my mother to ask how to cook onions, for example, and we would make onion soup.

In this area, Tal Afar or Mosul, people usually store grain and that is what they base their meals on. They might eat grain with onions or whatever they could find for a meal.

Meanwhile, insurgents were threatening the Sunni who constituted two-thirds of the population, warning them against selling food to the Shi'a minority.

The changes we were able to make may seem small, but we did what we could do as quickly as we could do it, and it was all accomplished under constant machine gun fire directed at the castle. The castle walls were dotted with loopholes, arrow slits for defenders to fire through. I'd put a helmet on the end of a rifle and raise it so that it could be seen from outside. It always drew fire, almost immediately. To this day, I never have seen what the town looks like from the top of the castle.

But help was on the way, this time in the person of LTC Christopher Hickey who would help to turn the tide in Tal Afar.

LTC Christopher Hickey, Harbinger and Instrument of Change

About ten days after we arrived at the castle, three or four Bradley APCs arrived with LTC Davis' replacement, Lieutenant Colonel Christopher Hickey. Hickey was friendlier, more personable than Davis. He also was open and more willing to talk. It was obvious that he had some background in Tal Afar. He asked incisive questions.

After I pointed out where the Sunnis live and the Shi'a, I showed him where the machine gun fire was coming from.

He asked me whether I was assigned to Tal Afar as punishment.

I said, "No. The police chief of Nineveh is my friend. He asked me to come here."

"So," he said, "your friend sent you to your death."

I said, "Only God decides whether we live or die, but the general trusts me and has confidence in me." Hickey looked at me a long moment before he said, "What can I do to help?"

That was the first real difference from the lieutenant colonel he replaced. Davis wanted change, but he never offered to help. Offering to help was Hickey's first instinct.

I said. "We need uniforms; all the police are in civilian clothes. And we need food. And our ammunition is exhausted."

He acted decisively. "Find a tailor and let him measure the policemen one by one and we will pay him to make their uniforms."

He had cases of water in the APCs. He gave us a number of them and some MREs (Meals, Ready to Eat) as emergency food.

I felt very comfortable with him; I thought, "This is a man who will work with me."

Two days later he brought a light machine gun, four or five AK-74s, and ammunition. He also met the tailor and assured him that he would pay for the uniforms.

We sat and talked through an interpreter about the situation in Tal Afar. LTC Hickey was a quiet, serious man, and when he talked I could sense his commitment, his excitement, and his eagerness to help. He clearly took his mission to heart.

But uniforms were not enough to make professional police officers. We had a great hall in the castle, where I gathered as many of our officers as I could to conduct training in how to be respectful, how to honor human rights, how to salute, and how to use weapons correctly and safely.

The police force comprised about 80 Shi'a officers. It was difficult to recruit Sunni because al -Qaeda, who lived among them, vowed to kill any Sunni who joined the police force.

The uniforms were soon ready, and they immediately made a difference in how the officers were perceived, not only by others but also in how they saw themselves. The uniform seemed to bolster self-respect. Now, when people visited the castle, they saw a uniformed police presence.

When LTC Hickey came, he appeared astonished at the transformation. Officers in neat uniforms presented respectful salutes. I took him to the hall and explained how we conducted training.

He seemed impressed with the rapid and demonstrable improvement, and the change seemed to make him more determined to help because he saw that it was making a difference. His visits became more frequent; he wanted to understand us better so that he could better support us.

He later said that I had a different personality, a charisma, he said, that distinguished me from previous police chiefs.

With a more reliable and professional police force, we were able to allow the prisoners—who suffered from malnutrition and a host of health issues often related to their mistreatment—to leave their cells for some sun and exercise. With LTC Hickey's support, we also were able to improve the food, and he brought medicine to treat the prisoners.

I asked his advice about how to pressure local judges to be more readily involved with the police. He brought the mayor to visit and it soon became clear that one of the causes of sectarian antagonism and violence in Tal Afar had been having a Shi'a police chief and a Sunni mayor.

~~~~

As LTC Hickey and I talked with the mayor, it was clear that he began to notice the differences between us, the effect of a significant difference in education and culture.

Hickey said that a serious problem with the mayor is that he never finished a meeting. And when we met, he never proposed a solution or made a suggestion; he only complained about the situation as it was.

As our relationship grew increasingly stronger, we met with increasing frequency and began to prepare ourselves for the work of making significant change in war-torn, terrorist-riddled Tal Afar.

7 Taming Tal Afar

"I am Iraqi."

Making Peace with the Sunni

My relationship with Lieutenant Colonel Hickey grew stronger day by day. I told him that we had to improve the lines of communication with the Sunni. We needed to be able to communicate with them as easily as we communicated with the Shi'a. Al-Qaeda prohibited Sunni from talking to U.S. forces or me, the chief of police, on pain of death.

We agreed that we had to find a way to improve relations with the Sunni. At the very least, we had to find a way for at least some Sunni representatives to talk with us, despite al -Qaeda's ban. They were allowed to talk to the mayor because he was friendly—and, we suspected complicit— with al -Qaeda.

The Sunni parts of the city did not respond to the government in any real way. Al-Qaeda controlled the city; al-Qaeda was their government. They controlled the hospital; they provided care for Sunni who were sick or wounded, and they denied treatment to the Shi'a. For their medical care, Shi'a depended on one doctor and one nurse in the neighborhood, but the hospital belonged to al-Qaeda.

Al-Qaeda recruited by bribery and promises. They started with small rewards. For example, they would promise $15 to a child if he reported on Americans or police locations or activity. They would give them $15 to tell them when the Americans or police were coming. And then they paid a little more for something a little more substantial, until, gradually, they would promise enough to plant a cell phone rigged to explode or to become a suicide bomber.

There were reports that al-Qaeda killed Shi'a who came to the hospital. There also were reports that they sometimes surgically implanted explosives in the bodies of dead Shi'a so that when they were claimed by relatives, the explosives would detonate, killing their friends or family. I did see one example of a corpse—the corpse of a young boy—that contained an IED that killed his father when he tried to pick up the body.

I stayed as neutral as I could. I didn't know anyone when I arrived in Tal Afar, so when they asked whether I was Shi'a or Sunni, I said, "I am Iraqi." Colonel Hickey liked that.

Enter H.R. McMaster

After about two months, LTC Hickey returned to the castle with another officer, Colonel H.R. McMaster. Colonel McMaster was—and remains—completely bald. He also is affable, wise, and kind, with a quick sense of humor. At the time I didn't realize that my new friend and ally was the same Colonel McMaster who led the American tanks, artillery, and ground troops that entered Iraq to begin the ground war when I was serving in al Basra in 2001.

The three of us had lunch and talked in an operations room I had set up in the castle. We had maps that showed Sunni and Shi'a neighborhoods, where the hot spots—trouble spots—were, where the terrorist cells were.

About an hour before the Americans left the castle, Col. McMaster said that he would return to Tal Afar with a brigade of U.S. troops in a month.

After Col. McMaster's arrival, events seemed to move quickly. LTC Hickey took me to meet some officers from Iraq's 3rd Division outside of the city. We went to al Kissnik, about 15 miles north of Tal Afar, and to Kassel, maybe five miles north.

After a few months in Tal Afar, I told Hickey that I had decided to take a vacation. I missed my wife and children, who were in Kurdistan. I had not seen them since coming to Tal Afar. Although they were only about three hours away, security concerns related to continuous and heavy insurgent activity made leaving the city as difficult and dangerous as entering it. Entering and leaving were so perilous that LTC Hickey had organized a plainclothes security squad to collect intelligence, carry messages, and bring food into the city.

General Ahmed, the provincial chief of police, authorized seven days of vacation, and he arranged for security to escort me out of the city.

Shortly after I arrived at Dohuk to see my family, I saw Bayan Jabr, Iraq's Minister of the Interior, on television. Police and border patrol fall under that ministry. The minister announced that Tal Afar's police chief had been fired for abandoning the city to the insurgents who now controlled it.

(The Ministry of the Interior was no stranger to controversy or political intrigue. In October of that year—2005—the ministry was accused of assassinating Saddam Hussein's defense lawyer. In December, *The Washington Post* reported that the Ministry of the Interior was embroiled in scandal when U.S. forces found widespread abuse and torture of prisoners held in two MOI detention centers. In 2006, the ministry admitted to having death squads.)

When I saw the minister announce that I had been fired, I called General Ahmed to ask what was going on. He said, "He's out of his mind. Don't worry about what he said, but you will have to cut your vacation short and return to Nineveh."

I was never able to prove it, but I have always believed that Ismael, the former police chief—the one I replaced—had started the rumor that I had abandoned the city. I also believe that he was working with the mayor who wanted him to return as police chief, even though they didn't like each other, because they both sympathized with the insurgents.

Until we could resolve the situation, Ahmed said to play along, to give the old police chief all of my files, to turn in my weapons, and to return to Mosul to work with him at Provincial police headquarters during the interim. I did as he said and returned to Mosul. The translator in Tal Afar later told me that LTC Hickey had been visibly angry about my being removed.

When I saw LTC Hickey again, he asked me what happened. I told him that it appeared that the interior minister had fired me. I think that Col. Hickey thought that I had quit because the job was exhausting and dangerous.

He asked, "Who will take your place?"

I told him that I had heard that Ismael would be restored to the position, and that I had been told to turn over my files and weapons to him.

Hickey paused, looking intently at me. ""Did they want you to leave or did you want to?"

I said, "I don't want to go. I am with you. Always."

Hickey met with Ismael and asked, "You want to be chief of police here? You had a lot of trouble with the mayor and with the people who live here."

"I will do better," Ismael said. "I will cooperate with the mayor."

Hickey was direct. "The mayor doesn't like you. He says that you are corrupt."

Ismael said, "What? What does he know? He is a dog! He is evil!"

Hickey asked, "Is that how you show that you will cooperate? By slandering him? If you say these things openly to me, how can you work with him? Stay here. We will talk again tomorrow."

Hickey returned to his unit, and that night BG Ahmed called me to say that he had talked to his contacts in Baghdad. "Stay in Tal Afar, General Najim," he said. "The American forces want you to stay and the interior minister agrees."

So I returned to Tal Afar, and the uncomfortable situation actually seemed to strengthen my relationship with Hickey. When we met with some Sunni citizens of Tal Afar, they said that after only two months with Hickey and me they could see the quality of life in Tal Afar improve. We told them that we planned to do much more, but we needed their help.

Shortly after that, the American 3rd ACR (Armored Cavalry Regiment) under the command of Col. McMaster occupied the Tal Afar Airport, seven or eight miles out of town, to begin Operation Restoring Rights.

8   Hickey and McMaster: Brothers in Islam

"... don't talk to their minds; talk to their hearts."

Col. McMaster, LTC Hickey, and I met with both Sunni and Shi'a sheikhs[1] outside of the city. For their safety, we always met with Sunni leaders outside of Tal Afar, because meeting at the castle would have been a death sentence for them, and the Shi'a sheikhs always knew when we met with the Sunni, so we had to do the same with them so that they saw we treated them equally.

I suggested a strategy to Col. McMaster and LTC Hickey: McMaster should cultivate a relationship with the Sunni; Hickey with the Shi'a. But I cautioned them: "Please, don't talk to their minds; talk to their hearts. That is the Arab way; that is how to reach them."

I knew that that stratagem had proven successful before, when al-Qaeda had been reluctant to attack Gen Casey because U.S. forces had spread the word that Gen. Casey's [Army General George W. Casey, the four-star general who, in 2004, replaced LTG Ricardo Sanchez as the top coalition commander in Iraq] grandfather was from the Sunni city of Ramadi. During the Clinton-Bush election there was a rumor that Bill Clinton's grandmother was from Mosul, and when he won the election, the people celebrated by firing rifles into the air because someone of Iraqi descent had been elected.

So, LTC Hickey made himself especially accessible to the Shi'a, and Col. McMaster to the Sunni so both sects could see that they had an ally and advocate.

Col. McMaster is very clever; he embraced my advice about talking to the people's hearts and told them, "I am Sunni, like you."

The Sunni told Col. McMaster that the police were corrupt. McMaster assured them that the new chief of police was sincerely trying to improve life in Tal Afar for everyone. "We trust him," he

---

[1]   An Arab leader, especially the chief or head of an Arab tribe or village.

said. "You have to have faith in his reforms."

I promised that I would fire anyone I found guilty of practicing sectarian prejudice, abuse of power, or excessive force. I had to ensure that the new police remained above reproach. There would be no second chances if the people of Tal Afar thought that nothing had changed and began to mistrust us.

As another safeguard and proof of the integrity of the police, I promised to install judges at a castle outside of the city so that anyone who had a complaint could feel safe in going to the judges who had the authority to act on information they found true.

Within a few days, we had judges from Mosul, about 30 miles east, at the castle. We told the people of Tal Afar that they were free to make formal complaints—without fear of reprisal—about anyone or anything, whether the police, fellow residents, whatever. As a result of complaints that were determined to be founded, I fired some officers found guilty of wrongdoing.

When the U.S forces ordered Ismael to leave Tal Afar or be arrested, I talked with the Shi'a and the city council and said that they should counsel Ismael to go. I told them, "The U.S. forces are not playing. They will arrest him if he stays." That made some of the Sunni trust me and deepened my steadily-improving relationship with the U.S. forces.

LTC Hickey supplied steady meals for the Shi'a whose food supplies had been cut off. The Sunni had access to food from Russia, but they denied access to the Shi'a. Working with the U.S. forces, we appointed Shi'a food distributors and sent them to get food for the Shi'a section of town.

LTC Hickey also began to support schools in the isolated Shi'a area. For example, teachers often were not being paid because al-Qaeda intercepted the payroll coming from Mosul before it got to them. LTC Hickey arranged for an armed escort to protect the payroll.

As Hickey's relationship with the Shi'a deepened, so did McMaster's with the Sunni. We could see that we were making progress.

We collaborated with LTC Hickey to develop sources to gather intelligence within al-Qaeda cells. We began to plan and execute combined operations with Iraqi national police and the Iraqi army, which had assigned a company to stay in the Tal Afar castle.

The road to improving conditions in Tal Afar was not without obstacles or setbacks. For example, a Shi'a sheikh, Ali Haddi, whose brother was the deputy minister of the interior, lived near the Sunni area and tried to maintain relations with Sunni.

One time, when a Sunni leader was released from jail, Ali Haddi took his son to visit him in Sarai, a Sunni neighborhood. But the sheikh's older son and some other men came to the castle to tell us that al-Qaeda had killed Sheikh Ali and his son when he went to the Sunni neighborhood, and they were unable to retrieve their bodies.

From the castle, I could see a crowd gathering near the Sunni area, trying to retrieve his body, but they were unable to enter.

I got my bodyguards, Lt. Bassan, and five or six others to go out to help them, and Hickey sent helicopters to provide air support in case al-Qaeda attacked while we were trying to retrieve the bodies.

Al-Qaeda initially offered some resistance, but they withdrew when they realized that they could not prevail against American helicopters and my security forces, and we were able to bring their bodies home.

Briefing the Coalition

One day, an American convoy arrived at the castle unannounced. It was Col. McMaster, who said that he had come to take me to his headquarters at the airport. We arrived at 3rd ACR headquarters to find LTC Hickey waiting on the runway with maps of Tal Afar prominently displayed on stands. Shortly after we arrived, a small plane landed, and I saw the minister of the interior, who had recently appeared on television to announce a major offensive to clean up Tal Afar within three or four weeks. With him was General George Casey, then the commander of Coalition Forces in Iraq, whom I recognized from television.

The senior officials assembled in front of the maps and Col. McMaster briefed them on the situation in western Nineveh and then he said, "Now General Najim, chief of police in Tal Afar, will brief you on the situation in that city."

Although I was not forewarned, as a career military officer, I felt quite comfortable briefing General Casey. I pointed out where the Sunni lived and the Shi'a areas and I showed the location of the castle and where we knew there were pockets of al-Qaeda operatives who denied the Shi'a food, medicine, and medical care. Shi'a were dying from minor wounds that went untreated. We explained that we relied on U.S. convoys to transport the wounded out of the city for medical care, and that, thanks to Hickey, we were able to smuggle food into the Shi'a neighborhoods.

The city was a ghost town, I told them, with Sunni mortars raining down throughout the day, and the constant sound of machine gun fire. As a result, we saw two or three fatal casualties and six or seven wounded among the Shi'a every day.

I made clear that the police force relied completely on U.S. forces for support and provisions: food, ammunition, etc. The local government provided nothing.

I saw the change in the interior minister, who said that he had a better understanding of what was happening in Tal Afar. General Casey also seemed satisfied with the briefing.

After the briefings, we toured the city by helicopter and I pointed out the various areas I had indicated in maps during my briefing. When we returned to 3rd Division headquarters we met with additional Iraqi and U.S. representatives, including BG Ahmed; the governor of Mosul, Derait Keshmoud; the commander general of the Kashid Iraq division and his staff officers; the minister of defense; and General David Rodriguez, who was then the commander of the American division in Mosul. The commander of the Iraqi division and his staff also gave a briefing on Tal Afar.

Over the protests of the Iraqi officers who said that it would take three or four months...or more, the interior minister repeated his promise to clean up Tal Afar in three or four weeks. He would not be moved: He said, "I want it done in weeks, not months."

All agreed that the people of Tal Afar had suffered enough. They were starving; they endured continuous fighting; and now, the minister had promised them hope that that would all change in three or four weeks. We were anxious about how it would affect them when it didn't happen. Over all loomed the awareness that the terrorists had returned almost immediately after two previous missions in the city, and we had to know that this time we could clear them out so completely that they could not get a toehold again. Al-Qaeda still controlled the city, but we didn't believe that they were strong enough to hold it.

When the defense minister said that he didn't understand why the chief of police of one city was briefing senior leaders on the insurgency situation, Gen. Casey gave me a challenge coin[2] and said "Don't worry." He seemed quite comfortable with me and I had the feeling that he had heard about me from the American forces

---

[2]   A coin bearing a unit or organization identification as evidence of membership.

and knew that he could trust me.

When we returned to the airport, we talked with Col. McMaster and LTC Hickey who both seemed pleased with the way the meetings had gone, but we agreed that we needed to spend more time talking with the sheikhs, both Shi'a and Sunni leaders.

When I returned to my office, one of the Sunni with whom I had begun to develop a relationship was waiting for me. He already knew everything that had transpired at the briefings from which I had just returned. Before I could return to my office, someone at the briefing had fully reported the discussions to al-Qaeda.

I think that some Iraqi officers believed that it was prudent to have a good relationship with al-Qaeda, both for personal reasons and to keep at least the appearance of security. My Sunni contact told me that al-Qaeda was furious that I had been among those who insisted that months to clear them out would be too long, that the time frame had to be shorter.

When I told Col. McMaster about al-Qaeda knowing all the details of our meetings, he said that with so many people attending the conferences, we had to assume that there would be leaks. We had to assume that al-Qaeda would be privy to all of our discussions, to any plans that we make.

Strengthening the Police Force

As I mentioned earlier, the police force was entirely Shi'a because al-Qaeda had threatened the lives of Sunni who joined, so the only way to balance the police force Shi'a with Sunni was to recruit outside of Tal Afar.

General Ahmed gave me permission to hire 500 Sunni police officers because al-Qaeda had intimidated any local Sunni who considered joining. I brought as many new police as I could find from outside the area. Tensions between Sunni and Shi'a were not as high outside of Tal Afar. Bringing in the outside Sunni made the police force more balanced, and the Sunni officers from outside of Tal Afar were more objective, less likely to choose sectarian sides.

Day by day we gained more and more control of the city. We also implemented a new plan of sending daily reports to Mosul about casualties, hostile action, and al-Qaeda activity in the city.

9   Police Chief and Mayor: A Bloodless Coup

"He continued to have influence, and he continued to be corrupt."

In June or July of 2005, LTC Hickey came to me and said, "General, I am not comfortable with the mayor. I don't trust him. It makes me uneasy that he is safe driving his car alone in Tal Afar. I don't understand why al-Qaeda allows him safe passage, unless, as we have heard, he is involved with them."

Hickey continued, "I think that we need to replace the mayor. He only holds city council meetings in Sunni areas. We need a mayor for everyone."

The governor of Mosul agreed. He said that the mayor of Tal Afar doesn't understand that he is not only the mayor of Sunni. A few days later, the governor told the mayor that he had evidence that the mayor was working with al-Qaeda, so he wanted him to resign. "If you don't resign," he said, "I will have you arrested."

At the same time. the citizens also made clear that they wanted Ismael out of the city. Although he was no longer the chief of police, he continued to have influence and he continued to be corrupt.

I tried to think of good people to replace the mayor. I said, "Brigadier Said from the old army lives in Tal Afar. Said might want to be mayor. I'll ask him if he is interested."

LTC Hickey looked at me silently before saying, "I think that you are the best person to be mayor."

"No," I said. "I am a military man. I came here to be chief of police. I am not even from Tal Afar and the city charter requires that the mayor be from the city."

"The Sunni seem comfortable with you," LTC Hickey said. "And the

Shi'a also seem comfortable with you. I think that you are the best choice for mayor."

Up this point, the Sunni thought I was Shi'a and the Shi'a thought that I was Sunni. I would only declare myself Iraqi.

I understood that the U.S. forces wanted me to take the job, but I didn't like the idea. Iraq is not like a little United States. In Iraq, military rank is far more prestigious than political position. A general officer is far more important than a mayor.

The city council and the U.S. Army representatives both said that it was time to name a new mayor. City council said, "But no one wants it. It is too dangerous."

The U.S. Army said, "Then name someone from city council." City council said no. It is too dangerous.

LTC Hickey urged me to take the job. He said that he would help me; he'd be an adviser, a sort of silent partner. "You can accomplish a lot as chief of police," he said, "but the mayor has more power and authority and can accomplish so much more."

"More to the point," he said, "both the Sunni and the Shi'a accept you."

Again I reminded him that I am not from Tal Afar. The mayor must be a resident of the city.

Soon after, two members of Nineveh's provincial council met in the castle with the city council. It was a long discussion. At the end, they had decided that I should be mayor, and they voted to appoint me, without objection.

So it happened that I became mayor and continued to run the police department as well. The biggest problem in the city was security. BG Sabbah served as my deputy. He also was from outside of Tal Afar, but I have known him well since we served together in Air Defense in Saddam's army.

By that time, we had no police officers from the city. They refused to join the security forces. After 2007, when the insurgents were gone, the city was peaceful, and the danger had passed, local men who had been police officers before al-Qaeda controlled Tal Afar said that they should be rehired. They argued that they should be getting the salaries that were going to the outsiders I had recruited, the police who had done the hard work of taming the city. But we stayed with those who had taken the job when it was most difficult and dangerous.

With strong support from the American forces, as mayor I was able to accomplish more than suppressing the terrorists. The infrastructure had been allowed to deteriorate for years. The water and sewage system was clogged and crumbling from neglect. We repaired and rebuilt the system to return it to service and we improved the electricity grid so that that Tal Afar had continuous power. In most of Iraq it continues to be unreliable.

10 Operation Restoring Rights

"The Maghaweer.. began shouting anti Sunni slogans, which incited the Sunnis."

The Coming Battle

We applied pressure at the provincial level and Nineveh Province provided the city with gas and fuel. We also met with Sunni and Shi'a sheikhs, the deputy prime minister, the minister of defense, and other central government figures in Baghdad to discuss how to improve conditions in Tal Afar.

Maybe most important of all, we liberated the hospital from the insurgents' grasp and induced the Iraqi army to secure and hold the medical facilities. For the first time in modern memory, Shi'ites had access to medical care at the Tal Afar hospital.

I met frequently with the heads of all of the city's departments, water, hospital, education, etc. Sometimes we held the meetings at the 3rd Army headquarters. Al-Qaeda always knew through Sunni sheikhs when the meetings were scheduled, and they urged the sheikhs to persuade Americans and Iraqis not to mount operations against them. Some Sunni sheikhs feared retribution for attending the meetings when they returned to the city.

The deputy prime minister asked the sheikhs to condemn terrorism. The Shi'a sheikhs were willing, but the Sunni sheikhs who lived among the terrorists were afraid to do so.

We planned the Tal Afar operation at 3rd Armored Cav. headquarters. During these meetings we agreed that any operations in Tal Afar must be meticulously planned well in advance to protect the residents and to deny insurgents the propaganda fodder that would result from any missteps or innocent casualties.

We finally reached an agreement: If al-Qaeda continued to target

71

civilians and disrupt services the sheikhs would be obliged to denounce the actions and support raids against the terrorist group. The Sunni sheikhs were nervous. They insisted that we distinguish between resistance and terrorism, between armed assaults on civilians and children, hospitals and schools, and armed assaults on military, police, or other state actors.

No matter what they called it, it isn't resistance if the targets are civilians or children. No matter how often they repeat it, it is not resistance, and we decided that a military operation was the only way to deal with the terrorists.

Clearing Tal Afar

When the 3rd ACR (Third Armored Cavalry Regiment) arrived, its commander, Col. H.R. McMaster, first moved to close the Iraqi/Syrian border to deny insurgents entry or escape. Toward the end of August, he ordered Alpha Company, 113th Engineer Battalion, to build an eight-foot berm dotted with military outposts and light machine guns around the 24-mile circumference of Tal Afar to prevent access by vehicles trying to avoid checkpoints on the roads leading into and out of the city.

We agreed to establish an evacuation camp outside of the Sarai neighborhood, where al-Qaeda was concentrated.

Following the example I had seen work so effectively in al Basra, Colonel McMaster deployed 6,000 Iraqi troops to partner with his U.S. troops, and U.S. and Iraqi Special Forces, to begin clearing the neighborhoods, evacuating citizens to temporary camps while troops conducted a house-to-house search for weapons and terrorists. National and Mosul police provided perimeter security and controlled access to main roads.

As troops began the house-to-house search, they encountered intense resistance from the insurgents. U.S. attack- and scout helicopters guided troops from the air and tracked terrorists as they sought refuge. The helicopters also provided ground-troop support when the terrorists engaged our troops in firefights.

I told Col. McMaster that, to forestall al-Qaeda attacks, I thought it was important to maintain an American military presence in the city after clearing the insurgents. The U.S. soldiers were better trained and more professional than Iraqi troops. We also needed security to

72

supervise the police officers who manned checkpoints with Iraqi troops. He agreed and posted troops in small outposts throughout the city.

We had to be very careful to protect our citizens. Of course it was our responsibility to do so, but it also was critical for them to see us as their allies and protectors so that they would willingly join the fight against al-Qaeda. We had to guard against abuse and provocation and to ensure their safety at hospitals and in the castle.

To my knowledge, Col. McMaster was the sole U.S. voice for keeping U.S. Army troops in the city. In the face of strong opposition, he returned to the United States in 2005 to seek the support of Vice President Richard Cheney.

I told General Rodriguez[3], "I don't want what happened in Fallujah to happen in Tal Afar." [During the 1991 Gulf War, two attempts, one British and one Coalition, to destroy a bridge across the Euphrates River in Fallujah, resulted in about 200 civilian deaths when they hit crowded market places instead.] I told him that I would not tolerate the use of artillery or jet fighters against the city. I said, "Consider the first artillery shell that lands in Tal Afar my resignation. I won't say anything more. The shell itself is my resignation."

"Fighter jets will kill innocent civilians," I said. "No matter how accurate artillery fire is, it will kill innocent civilians. The death of innocent civilians is not acceptable."

General Rodriguez asked how I expected him to support our ground troops without artillery or fighter jets. I said "Helicopters are far more accurate. The pilots have more time to target the enemy and protect civilians. They can provide support for the ground troops"

I told him how we had cleared Basra, systematically and safely, and the general promised not to use artillery or fighter jets.

We planned the operation for September.

Without consulting me or the U.S. forces, the Iraqi minister of the interior deployed General Rasheed Iflay and a Maghaweer al-Dakhiliah regiment from Baghdad. Although they are called special forces, the Maghaweer al-Dakhiliah are Interior Ministry officers,

---

[3]   Major General David Rodriguez, then commander of the Multinational Force in Iraq

poorly trained and poorly disciplined police in military uniforms.

The Maghaweer joined a Shi'a regiment and began shouting anti-Sunni slogans, which incited the Sunnis. I began receiving reports of the unrest and its cause and the media quickly picked up on reports of sectarian troops in Tal Afar.

This sudden disturbance proved another occasion for Col. McMaster to demonstrate his intelligence and wisdom. First, he ordered an urgent message to the minister of the interior to withdraw the Maghaweer without delay. When the minister refused and the people grew increasingly angry and agitated, Col. McMaster went to General Iflay and told him that if he did not withdraw his troops within 24 hours, U.S. troops would consider them enemy agents and respond accordingly. His tone and expression left no doubt that he was serious.

The troops were quickly withdrawn, which was especially important because it strengthened confidence in Col. McMaster and me and proved to the citizens of Tal Afar beyond a reasonable doubt that we were not sectarian partisans.

Finally, we brought in auxiliary police from a reserve regiment in Mosul to supervise security in the camps and to suppress sectarian violence.

11   The Battle of Tal Afar

"... the fear of Retribution by Al -Qaeda was very real and always present."

The battle for the insurgent-controlled city of Tal Afar in Nineveh Province was the culmination of my career as an Iraqi military officer. It was a role I neither sought nor anticipated. When I accepted the job as police chief of the lawless city, I had no inkling of the historic role our decisions in rooting out al-Qaeda and taking back control of the sprawling city would play in the future of Iraq.

When I was the mayor of Tal Afar, a city in Nineveh Province, about 50 km (31 miles) west of Mosul and 200 km (124 miles) north of Kirkuk, the population was between 200,000 and 250,000. By 2007, the population had dropped to about 80,000, almost all Turkmen, 60,000 of whom are Sunni Muslims, the remaining 20,000, Shi'ites.

The Battle of Tal Afar in September 2005, was a U.S.–led joint operation to destroy the insurgents' unchallenged hold on Tal Afar. The official strategy, called "clear, hold, and build" was to clear the city of insurgents; hold or retain control; and build strong, democratic institutions, targeted reconstruction, and economic infrastructure. The city's proximity to the Syrian border had made it a safe haven and base of operations for terrorists, foreign and domestic.

Despite heavy fighting, our strategy and meticulous planning resulted in minimal casualties. The operation officially ended on September 18.

As police chief and mayor, I was able to closely observe American soldiers and officers showing compassion for my countrymen. They were not the demons, the bogeymen of my countrymen's nightmares. They were decent men and women trying to do the best they could in a perilous and chaotic situation.

I found they were willing—eager even—to listen to the counsel of an Iraqi leader who treated them as colleagues in rebuilding the country, rather than as invaders. They were attentive to sincere advice and guidance, particularly when that leader showed that he was willing to risk his life alongside the Coalition forces risking theirs.

Tal Afar, which the U.S. military often called "a second Fallujah" because of the widespread destruction and violence, became the setting for Coalition forces to begin to know the character of Iraqis as people and as allies. It was a transformative experience, a crossroads that opened new paths to understanding and cooperation.

I see the collaborative efforts in Tal Afar as a turning point for post-Saddam reconstruction, but not in a vacuum.

Al-Qaeda tried hard to tarnish the image of the operation with accusations of misconduct and abuse, but the media had been present throughout, and the public had seen the unprecedented lack of harm to people or property during and after the operation.

Not long after the operation concluded, a half-dozen car bombs exploded in Baghdad and Babylon. Abu Musab al Zarqawi, al-Qaeda's leader in Iraq, claimed responsibility for them and announced that they were in retaliation for the defeat of al-Qaeda in the Battle of Tal Afar.

As we had done in Basra, we used "identifiers" in Tal Afar, informants willing to point out those they knew to be terrorists. We questioned the suspected terrorists, but when Col. McMaster, LTC Hickey, and I met with Sunni sheikhs, they told us that most of the young men in custody were innocent.

After three or four days, in fact, we released most of the captured suspects. The others were held in the custody of the Iraqi army or in civilian prisons.

When the sheikhs told us that many of our identifiers were liars, falsely identifying young men to impress U.S. officials or settle old scores, Col. McMaster and LTC Hickey decided to test them.

They had American translators of Iraqi ancestry and unquestioned loyalty photographed. These were young men who had lived in the United States all their lives and had been brought to Iraq as trusted interpreters. Their photos were included in the array of suspected terrorists.

Some of the identifiers picked out men we knew to be beyond reproach, free of suspicion. One of the identifiers was especially credible when he appeared to become very excited, practically jumping up and down. He pointed at a picture and said, "I know him personally. He is the most dangerous terrorist in Tal Afar. "

The terrorist he identified was an Arab-American interpreter I knew and considered a friend. He had lived in the United States for most of his life.

Those who failed the test were dismissed.

When we had cleared most, if not all, of the terrorists following the Battle of Tal Afar, the American troops were stationed at small outposts throughout city. For the first time ever, anywhere in Iraq, Americans were living in neighborhoods among the people of Tal Afar. We had two American regiments living in the city, and LTC Hickey moved into the castle, a few rooms away from where I lived and worked.

This integration of U.S. troops among Iraqis was a distinct and significant milestone, and the results, in terms of stopping the sectarian fighting and minimizing the abuse of civil rights by Iraqi security personnel was considerable and almost immediate.

No longer constantly watched by al-Qaeda, the people of Tal Afar were free to meet and talk with American soldiers, and that growing familiarity helped to build trust and confidence in the American forces.

When the Battle of Tal Afar was over and peace had returned to the city for the first time in many years, Prime Minister Ibrahim al-Jaafari came to see the results of the four-day operation.

General Casey took him to the 3rd Iraqi Division at Al-Kissik Military Base, northwest of Mosul, where I met with the prime minister to describe the strategy we used in Tal Afar, especially how and why the operation was more successful than we had hoped.

"Colonel McMaster was a maestro," I told him, "and the American forces, Iraqi police, and Iraqi army were his well-tuned orchestra, not an off-note among them. The outcome was all we hoped for, far better than the result of the Fallujah operation with the same mission, to root out and destroy al-Qaeda and its allies. We had no loss of property—not a building was damaged—and we suffered fewer than a dozen deaths, civilian, military, and police combined. It was a great success and a shining example of what can be accomplished when Iraqi and Coalition security forces genuinely cooperate in planning and executing an operation."

Iraqis had learned—not without reason—to be mistrustful of Coalition forces. In Tal Afar we had worked hard to overcome that mistrust and to forge an alliance that was based on a deeper understanding than government-government or military-military. We were connecting at a basic human level, working to win hearts, not minds. We did not treat the citizens of Tal Afar as the enemy, as suspected terrorists, but as our brothers and sisters, and we strove to protect them.

Because the prime minister was also a medical doctor, I used the metaphor of a skilled surgeon operating on a seriously-ill patient. It was important to excise the cancer without damaging the healthy tissue. So it was in Tal Afar. We had set out to remove the insurgents without harming innocent people, so we wielded a scalpel, not a butcher knife.

As the patient must regain his strength, now came the time for Tal Afar to rebuild, to heal. It was time for the patient to recover. It would not be all at once, but gradual, and Tal Afar was ready for the healing to begin. For that to occur, I told him, "I need to retain control of the police and the Iraqi troops that remain in the city."

He agreed. As prime minister, al-Jaafari was also commander-in-chief of the Iraqi military. When I was named police chief, I was also reactivated as a military officer and promoted to brigadier general. Now he said, "I am promoting you to major general and the troops in Tal Afar will remain under your command, as will the police."

The prime minister added that he intended to give Tal Afar $100 million of the foreign aid [Iraq] had received to begin the work of rebuilding the city. He would begin with $50 million. The prime minister named then-minister of interior, now speaker of Iraq's Parliament, Osama al-Nujaif, brother of Atheel Nujaif, the exiled governor of Nineveh Province, as director of the Tal Afar rebuilding committee.

The concept of a rebuilding committee was well-intentioned, but none of the directors lived in Tal Afar, and rebuilding the city was not a priority for them. During my tenure, we never received a dollar of the promised money from the central government.

However, Col. McMaster and LTC Hickey were determined to leave Tal Afar better than they had found it, and, despite the central government's failure to deliver on its promises, the work that we had begun together continued. We established the Brotherly Dialogue Committee, a council of Shi'a and Sunni sheikhs, and we encouraged dialogue between them.

It was difficult to persuade many of the Sunni sheikhs to participate in the council. The fear of retribution by al-Qaeda was very real and always present. The committee started with three Sunni sheikhs: Qassim Farhad, Abdulnoor Obaidi, and Mohamed Hanash Halaibek. The Shi'ite sheikhs were Waliy Joulaq, Abdullah Moussawi, Hashim Antir, Mohammed al-Moula and Khalid Mohssin Habish.

We encouraged dialogue among the sheikhs, but we understood that we would have to begin with baby steps. The plan was not without problems.

One of the early obstacles was the list of Sunni on the watch list for wanted men at checkpoints. The extent of the list angered the sheikhs and caused resentment and unrest among the general Sunni population. We asked the sheikhs to go through the list and remove the names of anyone they would vouch for. We sought a consensus on which names were legitimately included and which were erroneous. Through the council, we were able to delete more than half the names on the wanted list.

We asked the Shi'a not to complicate the work of conciliation by forcing Sunni residents out of their neighborhoods, although some Shi'a were forced to leave Sunni neighborhoods.

We also asked the sheikhs to take several steps:

1. Encourage trade between Sunni and Shi'a, and reopen markets that had been closed during the clearing operation.
2. Actively encourage mixed Shi'a-Sunni marriages. To that end, our municipal government subsidized intermarriages.
3. Divide project contracts between Sunni and Shi'a to force them to cooperate with each other.

We found these simple measures to be so effective that they began to spread to other towns and cities.

The sheikhs were strong voices for reconciliation. Their work did much to transform Tal Afar and fully coalesce Shi'a and Sunni. I believe that the U.S. officials in the area recognized and appreciated their significant contributions to bringing peace to Tal Afar.

Time would prove that the sheikhs who courageously agreed to serve on the Brotherly Dialogue Committee were staking their lives on the outcome. In 2008, al-Qaeda assassinated Abdullah Moussaoui and Mohammed al-Moula at the home of Falah Farhad, another Sunni sheikh, in Mosul. Although Farhad escaped death at the time, he also was later assassinated.

LTC Hickey and I worked together so closely that we could read each other with a glance. When we were in meetings, each could look at the other and understand what he wanted.

For example, when we were in a meeting that was becoming contentious, a mere look told him that I thought he needed to be less confrontational, to let some minor points slide so that we could concentrate on major points. Similarly, I knew from a look when he wanted me to change my demeanor or approach.

Friendlies Among the Foes

An initial problem with U.S. forces, understandable but damaging, was that it was hard to see the friendlies for the foes among the indigenous population. American forces were so focused on finding insurgents that they didn't see the civilians who wanted nothing more than to live in peace. They disregarded the people among whom al-Qaeda lived, the people al-Qaeda threatened and intimidated, the people al-Qaeda used, both to blend in and to aid and abet them, on threat of death for themselves and their families.

Often it seemed that the Americans believed that all Iraqis were al-Qaeda. They treated them as enemies and remained oblivious to the effect of their contemptuous treatment on how Iraqis viewed and responded to them, with fear, anger, and resentment.

12   Counterinsurgency vs Conventional Warfare

"They feared the terrorists and were caught between them and the Coalition forces who saw no distinction between the enemy and innocent people struggling to survive."

Counterterrorism and counterinsurgency are not conducted the same way as conventional warfare. Conventional warfare is conducted on the battlefield with an identifiable enemy. Counterinsurgency is waged among innocents and non-combatants, people who live at the mercy of the terrorists who held them as hostages, without physical restraint. And it was impossible to tell which was which by looking at them. These unwilling accomplices were expendable to the insurgents and guilty by association in the eyes of counter-terrorists.

These reluctant allies might be victimized or involuntarily conscripted, their lives and the lives of their families in the balance, and the Americans, the enemies of the terrorists, considered the conscripts and families who unwillingly harbored the enemy, enemies themselves. The insurgents had no qualms about killing women and children to achieve their ends, and the innocents they terrorized into aiding and abetting them found themselves torn between two enemies. They feared the terrorists and were caught between them and the Coalition forces who saw no distinction between the enemy and innocent people struggling to survive.

Of course, the Coalition forces feared and mistrusted everyone, not always without justification, so the hardest task before us was teaching the Coalition forces in Nineveh, American forces, to learn to begin to trust innocent civilians, who were as much victims of the war as the troops who died in battle or the victims of terrorist attacks.

My advice to the U.S. troops was, "You cannot win by military might; you only can win through reaching their hearts. You must teach them that we are the good guys and that they can trust us, because if they do not separate from the terrorist willingly, they do not break from them for the long term."

Al-Qaeda's goal was to sow confusion and strife, to incite discontent and discord. They were expert at the concept of divide and conquer, and when their efforts are accompanied by car bombs and exploding buildings, these tactics work very well.

The innocent civilians needed to have their eyes open to the alternative, to perceive the American forces as hope instead of as a threat. The American armed forces, like most armed forces, rely mainly on firepower and military might. This battle for the soul of Iraq would only be won if we first won the hearts and minds of the populace through kindness and civility.

When I talked with civilians, I asked them whom they preferred. At first, our civilians hated the Americans more than Iraqi military or police, but over time, they welcomed the stabilizing presence of American troops.

The Americans began to introduce humanitarian services. They provided medical supplies for the sick and wounded, and books and toys for the children. They began to patronize local merchants, improving the merchants' economic situation while they got to know each other. As they came to know each other as people, trust began to outweigh suspicion.

The American troops also openly watched Iraqi soldiers to guard against abuse. Americans oversaw the city's construction contracts, so they were visible in improving the infrastructure and the quality of life in Tal Afar.

As I mentioned earlier, because of its close proximity to Syria, Tal Afar is a logical and convenient way station for insurgents crossing the border. Because of the density of terrorists who held Tal Afar, it was considered a safe haven for them.

Some of the terrorist leaders in Nineveh, including Abu Alaa, a senior leader of al-Qaeda in Iraq, lived in Tal Afar.

For many years, terrorists in Tal Afar created and maintained huge underground caches of weapons and supplies. These caches were so well-designed that they remained undetectable even by sophisticated U.S. ordnance detection, and hidden caches are being discovered to this day.

The city was a base of operations for terrorists who could meet, exchange information, and receive orders they were to carry out throughout Iraq. One of al-Qaeda's goals in Iraq was fomenting sectarian violence, so Shi'ites in a predominantly Sunni area were an easy target.

In the summer before the operation, a truck loaded with explosives was detonated in the Shi'a al Sada neighborhood near the castle. Twenty-four Shi'a were killed and another hundred or so wounded.

During the same summer, two suicide bombers caused many more casualties when they detonated car bombs in the al-Moualinneen neighborhood, which had been built to house Shi'a teachers.

The time for a major operation, "Operation Restoring Rights," later known simply as "The Battle of Tal Afar" was overdue.

During the summer before the operation, the deputy prime minister met with Sunni sheikhs from Tal Afar. Although they continued to refuse to publicly denounce terrorism, they did agree to pressure the terrorists to leave, and not to victimize the citizens of Tal Afar.

Before the operation, I publicly and officially notified the people of Tal Afar of the impending action. I recounted the increase in terrorist activity, the widespread damage to property, and the lives lost. I talked about how unnatural terrorism and sectarianism are, and I stressed the immediate need to cleanse the city of this blight, to clear the city of sectarian strife, for Shi'a and Sunni to live together in peaceful coexistence, as they had before the rise in sectarianism.

I reminded them that a basic tenet of Islam is that every person in the world is either a brother in religion or a human being created by the same God. Murder is wrong. As the Qur'an says: "To kill one innocent man or woman is to kill all of humanity; to save one human is to save all of humanity."

I used the opportunity to remind people of Tal Afar that we all trace our lineage to a single household with a Sunni brother and a Shi'a sister.

So I used both rational and emotional arguments to appeal to the people of Tal Afar. I also gave specific instructions to stay away from the farm area southwest of the city once the operation begins. Anyone found in the restricted area—a logical escape route for terrorists—would be considered a target.

Sarai was the only neighborhood from which we evacuated civilians, somewhere between 15,000 and 20,000 of them. Some had already left when they heard about the imminent operation, but we did everything possible to make them safe and comfortable while they stayed in the camp. Some left for nearby villages or stayed with friends or relatives in other sections of the city.

The operation began in the al-Qadisiyah section of the city, with a brigade from the 3rd Iraqi Division and a regiment from Kirkuk supporting the American 3rd Armored Cavalry Regiment.

Other than the Sarai section and a few pockets of resistance, we cleared the entire city in just a couple of days. In all the other neighborhoods, we took the residents to a central building, just as we had done in Basra.

Abu Musab al-Zarqawi, the al-Qaeda leader in Iraq who was responsible for a savage campaign of suicide bombings and beheadings, took to the radio waves to order al-Qaeda in Tal Afar to fight to the last drop of blood. He claimed that U.S. and Iraqi soldiers were raping the women in Tal Afar.

I also used the airwaves to refute his accusations, and I invited the media to come to Tal Afar to observe the operation first-hand. I assigned security officers to protect them, and we allowed them access to the hospital, where Zarqawi claimed the rapes were taking place, as they reported on the fight for the soul of Tal Afar.

It took an additional two days to clear Sarai; the whole operation was over in four. In the end, 80 terrorists were dead. The Americans expressed their surprise at the minimal civilian casualties of the Battle of Tal Afar, possible because we did not use artillery or fighter jets. In total, we lost four U.S. troops, eight Iraqi troops and seven civilians, three of whom were killed in the prohibited farm area.

Three other civilian deaths were attributed to al-Qaeda, two men and the young daughter of one who had not evacuated Sarai when ordered.

During the operation we captured a little more than 800 suspected terrorists and huge stores of weapons, ammunition, and explosives. Thankfully, unlike Fallujah, not one building was destroyed and casualties, although regrettable, were minimal. For years, people expressed their astonishment at the careful planning and meticulous execution of the surgical operation. For our part, we were especially thankful that the operation did nothing to provoke a hostile reaction.

13   Renewal Begins

"A coat of paint on schools is not enough to win people's hearts. We need to create something real and lasting...."

Once the people felt more secure—their greatest need, hope, and desire—they clamored for reconstruction and jobs.

Americans had built jails and police stations throughout the city. During one opening ceremony I said to LTC Hickey, "Ten, twenty, thirty years after you are gone, what will people remember when they think of you? Police stations and jail cells. Decades after the British came, Iraqis remember them—and smile—when they look at the bridges and universities they built."

"If you focus only on jails and police stations— that's how you will be remembered. A coat of paint on schools is not enough to win people's hearts. We need to create something real and lasting in the city, substantial reconstruction."

Apparently he took the idea back to his superiors, because we soon turned a new page, rebuilding the city that had been so long neglected. We began a program of rebuilding and renovation that would live in the memory of Tal Afar for generations to come.

We built a modern medical clinic, a beautiful new public library, and an impressive office for the mayor in the highest section of the castle, in the highest part of the city, a shining symbol of which citizens can rightly be proud.

We repaved the main roads and built new ones and we built sidewalks for pedestrian safety. In every school, we created up-to-date computer rooms to bring students into the age of technology and to allow them to interact with the world. Students in Tal Afar had internet access that surpassed that in bigger cities such as Mosul.

Building was continuous, giving the people exactly what they most wanted and needed, jobs and modernization.

I insisted that the city needed its own television station to keep our citizens informed in a timely manner and to dispel or refute the constant rumors. The Americans also saw the need and provided the television facility that is still in use.

I also worked with the American forces to train a SWAT [Special Weapons and Training] team, and we had them give a presentation to our local police.

We established our own command and control group. Every week we gathered representatives—the American commander and his staff, the Iraqi battalion commander and his staff, the chief of police and some of his officers—to review, monitor, and plan, to discuss current circumstances and how to solve major problems in the city: Where were terrorists hiding? What new intelligence was coming in? What response was required from each element of our security forces? What equipment would be required? What do we need from the central government? Who would be the lead in each action?

We also met weekly with the directors of all of the city services to seek solutions to the issues they faced. We invited our advisers from the U.S. forces to see where they might help.

From time to time, we met with all the school principals to talk about the importance of keeping teachers from proselytizing, or from criticizing the government and sowing discontent. It was not uncommon for teachers to undermine the governing authority, advocate sectarianism, or glorify terrorists, and we wanted principals to be proactive in deterring them from influencing students to tear the delicate fabric of our society.

Sometime principals would tell us that teachers were inciting students, and we would call in the teachers to talk with them, to try to reason with them, to encourage them to change. When we were unsuccessful, we had to remove them.

I spent much of my time monitoring construction projects and talking with children. Both were important to the future of Tal Afar, but I believed that the children were the more important because the attitudes we instilled in them would determine the future of not only Tal Afar, but all of Iraq.

In the beginning, the children avoided American troops; they wouldn't shake hands with the soldiers, or look them in the eye. In time, as they began to trust and respect me as mayor, they saw my close relationship with the U.S. forces and they began to trust them, and they became comfortable with them, as well. Their attitude spread to their parents.

As Tal Afar grew stronger, we were able to offer at least modest help to some of the cities around us.

For example, deliveries from Mosul were constantly endangered by terrorists who killed, or threatened to kill, the drivers. They were especially determined to block medical supplies being delivered to Tal Afar.

The media were watching closely. At one point, the director of medical services in Mosul called me. He said that he was afraid to send medical supplies. "Please don't attack me in the media," he said. "The terrorists have said that they will kill me if I send help, and I have a family."

Fortunately, we had very good relations with Kurdistan from when the citizens of Tal Afar supported them against Turkish persecution. Although Mosul was silent, Tal Afar had demonstrations in the street protesting Turkey's attack on the autonomous region.

That the demonstrations took place in Tal Afar was significant. About 90% of the population were Turkmen, and when Turkey asserted that they were protecting the Turkmen in Kurdistan from being treating badly, the Turkmen in Tal Afar said that it was not true. They said, "Kurdistan supports us." When the Turks said that the peshmerga, or Kurdish militia, controlled Tal Afar, our citizens said, "There is no Kurdish militia presence in Tal Afar."

I had one other major advantage in rebuilding Tal Afar. Mayors in Iraq do not typically have engineers at their disposal. Similarly, the majority of city councils have no experience or expertise in city planning. With the help of the U.S. Forces in Nineveh, though, we contracted with new engineering graduates to work with us, to oversee and to advise us on rebuilding the city. In fact, I believe that Tal Afar was unique in having engineers dedicated to planning the rebuilding of the city. That does not mean that our rebuilding was free of problems.

Contracting in Iraq is not a transparent process. Unlike the United States government, which awards contracts based on strict specifications with close oversight, in Iraq, a government official might ask how much a project would cost. Say it was projected to cost $100,000, the man who gets the contract turns to a friend and says, "I need this project completed for $50,000." The friend says to his friend, "I will give you $25,000 to complete this project," and so on until they find the lowest cost anyone would accept to complete the project, maybe $10,000. Then the cut-rate sub-contractor goes about finding the cheapest materials and labor to complete the project. Of course, government officials had to receive their cut of the action, a kickback, from each of the contracts down the line.

We wanted the U.S. forces to oversee the contracts in Tal Afar, but we learned that even though the U.S. Government provided the funds, it did not provide oversight. They maintained that it was not the U.S. forces' role to supervise or enforce the contracts.

In the case of Tal Afar, my American associates and I would discuss our needs with our young engineers and the city council would then ask the Nineveh provincial council for the necessary funds. As I was determined to return Tal Afar to its former greatness, I took a personal interest in who received the contracts, the quality of the work, and accountability for the costs. As a result, our rebuilding in Tal Afar was of better design and better quality than was typical anywhere else in Iraq.

When I met with the prime minister I told him that we needed emergency funds to help the people who had suffered losses during the Battle of Tal Afar.

The prime minister provided $3.4 million, and we formed a committee of about 40 citizens, which I chaired. The committee decided how to allot the money. We allotted $200 assistance to each family, with additional money provided to families whose homes had been damaged so that they could make needed repairs. Another focus was the city's widows and orphans.

We understood that people who took pride in their homes, in their city, would take care of it. When damage isn't repaired, people begin to accept the increasing deterioration and they become demoralized.

We also understood that the city needed a committed leader. One who is committed to a goal can overcome any obstacle. I believed in the example of Mahatma Gandhi, who believed in the power of love. LTC Hickey and I regularly remained five to seven hours after meetings to talk with citizens who needed reassurance or help in understanding what we were doing. We also met with the most vocal groups to bring them together and to discourage factions from forming.

With all of the groups, I stressed their similarities and asked them why they would harm each other, how could they kill each other? I read many Surahs from the Qur'an to them. I quoted the Prophet, which had a powerful impact on people, and I emphasized that they were ultimately brothers, that in the end they all would be together.

LTC Hickey and I believed that we had a higher aim to establish a city in which people love, respect, and cooperate with each other. Always with that goal in mind, we accepted the obstacles and stumbling blocks as we kept our eyes on the greater goal.

The citizens of Tal Afar knew, with absolute confidence that we were with them in good times and bad. We were there to help whenever something happened, whatever happened. We were there in their darkest hours to find a way to alleviate their pain.

We wanted to be—and for them to see us as—their good servants there to help them. We wanted to help them, to support them, to smooth the way for them on the rough roads they found themselves traveling. They tried to protect us because they knew that we were protecting them.

Sometimes Sunni would call us and warn us not to go to a certain place because terrorists were planning to ambush us. One time, for example, they said, "They plan to have a suicide bomber approach you as a cripple on crutches."

This was a great gift to us from the people of Tal Afar.

Another way that the American forces made a long-term difference in Tal Afar was by helping us to harvest and store wheat. Our storage facilities had fallen into disrepair, and the Americans provided funds to rebuild the facilities, so we were able to provide our own wheat and to make our own flour and bread instead of relying on deliveries from Mosul. This was an especially important improvement for our Shi'a population who often were denied food imported by the insurgent-controlled Sunni, who saw a double advantage in both depriving their perceived foes of food and other staples and in driving a wedge between the haves and have-nots.

From about 1990 until now, the minister of trade imported food and basic goods from Russia—rice, sugar, flour, tea, tomatoes, lentils, beans, maybe 15 different items, even soap and laundry detergent—which he then distributed to the provinces for them to distribute among their towns and cities.

The first year that I was in Tal Afar, the Shi'a did not receive any of the Russian food or goods. After eight to ten months, though, we were able to begin diverting some of the Russian supplies to Shi'a families. Distributing the food more equitably also had the happy effect of significantly reducing the high prices of the black market trade in sugar, rice, etc.

We also assigned escorts, U.S. and Iraqi troops, to protect the drivers and ensure delivery of Russian food into the city.

We replaced most of the checkpoints that made life difficult and travel unpleasant with "check watching," posting police and military troops along the roads from Tal Afar to Mosul, Sinja, and Kurdistan to observe and provide additional security.

When I first arrived in Tal Afar, the streets were deserted during the hours of darkness, citizens afraid to walk abroad lest they fall prey to terrorist attacks or IEDs (improvised explosive devices). It took almost a year to make people comfortable walking after dark again, but then the streets again saw pedestrians and men sipping tea and talking at cafés after dark.

We returned order to Tal Afar and made it safer, but doing so required limiting some individual freedoms. For example suicide bombers almost always traveled alone, so we banned driving alone within the city limits. Everyone had to have at least one other person in the car. That law certainly made the Shi'a feel more secure, but the Sunni majority said that it was a serious inconvenience always to have someone else in the car.

We understood their objection, but we explained that sometimes individuals must sacrifice for the greater good to protect us from terrorism, from al-Qaeda.

Another way that we stymied al-Qaeda was by making it difficult to drive a stolen car. Al-Qaeda frequently stole cars, so we required citizens to attach identification plates to their windshields. At every checkpoint, sentries checked the driver's ID against the ID attached to the car to verify that this car belongs to this driver. When the IDs didn't match, we flagged the vehicle for investigation.

Drivers from outside the city needed a citizen to vouch for them and accompany them. If they did not know anyone in the city, we assigned a police officer to ride with them while they were there. It was a very effective measure against al-Qaeda's car bombs.

But simply preventing or reducing violence and destruction was not enough. We knew that we also had to move the city forward, to improve the quality of our citizen's lives. The American forces had some money to fund small projects in the city. As I mentioned earlier, contractors took almost everything we paid them for a project; very little filtered down to the laborers. I wanted everyone to be able to earn something, so I suggested that we use some of the American money to pay citizens to clean up their neighborhoods.

We set aside $5,000, and paid for each bag of trash brought to a collection point. A family could have old women, young children, and everyone in between collecting 1,000-2,000 Iraqi dinars, which was less than $1 or $2 USD, for each trash bag. Not only did the money—which seems like nothing to an American—mean a great deal to the families, but cleaning the streets also rebuilt pride in themselves and their city. People often are comfortable throwing trash in a street that is strewn with trash, less so on a street that is neat and clean. People who take pride in their neighborhood feel better about themselves and where they live. A small investment meant a great deal to the people and it helped them to take back their city.

We advertised the program on television, which worked well in Tal Afar, but as we had seen before with success, it didn't encourage other cities to follow our example. It made them jealous. The people in Mosul for example, became very upset. They asked why the mayor of Tal Afar could do that and the mayor of Mosul didn't do it for his people. Some sheikhs from Mosul said that they would "trade three mayors for Najim."

There finally came a time that it was impossible to find any trash to collect in Tal Afar.

I am Iraqi: blurring sectarian lines

LTC Hickey and I set out on a mission to visit every school in the city, armed with a pile of small gifts. I would ask children, "Are you Sunni or Shi'a?" and no matter which way they answered, I said, "I don't like that answer. Better than saying, 'I am Shi'a' or 'I am Sunni,' say 'I am Iraqi!'" Then when I asked again, "Are you Sunni or Shi'a?" they answered "Iraqi!" and we distributed gifts.

Before long, whenever I saw children on the street, they would shout, "I am Iraqi!"

I told the children, "When you are at home and you hear your mother or father say, 'I am Shi'a' or 'I am Sunni,' you should say, 'I don't like to hear you say that. Better you should say, "I am Iraqi!"'"

The notion of being Iraqi before being Shi'a or Sunni grew ever bigger in Tal Afar and spread to Mosul. I felt proud that I had begun to change the mindset of the people, at least in Nineveh. And I knew that it made a difference.

Despite the changing attitude, old habits do not disappear overnight, and many Sunni still feared repercussions if they were to work on government redevelopment projects. I gathered some of them around me and asked them, "How long? How long will you live in the shadow of al-Qaeda? How long will you live in fear?"

"Your Shi'a brothers are in a much better economic situation because they choose to work with the Americans. You need to kill the fear inside you and join them in renewing Tal Afar, in improving your economic status."

And they began to work with us, first one or two and then a few more and as the others saw that they were not harmed, the few became many, Sunni and Shi'a working side by side with the Americans to make Tal Afar a better place to live.

I thought that USAID (United States Agency for International Development) seriously miscalculated in telling Iraqis working on their projects that they should not tell anyone that they are working with Americans. They thought that if people knew they were working with Americans they wouldn't be willing to work. I believed that that policy was a mistake. I said, "Let people know that they are working on American projects and earning American money. Let them know that the Americans are creating jobs and rebuilding our city."

I felt strongly enough that I went on TV and announced that these were American projects. I wanted people to know that America had created so much work, so many improvements in Tal Afar.

But I had miscalculated, although not in the way USAID had feared. Instead of taking my point about how much the Americans had done to improve Tal Afar, people in other cities again became jealous of our progress.

Success is its own Punishment

As I mentioned above, and as is sadly common, when other cities heard of our success, rather than working to follow our example, they tried to spoil our success. Instead of clamoring for similar projects in their own towns, they pressured the provincial government: Why is Tal Afar getting all the projects? What about our town? Why is Tal Afar being treated better than we are?

The government in Mosul didn't know how to satisfy them, so they ordered me to stop all American projects in Tal Afar immediately.

I refused.

They threatened to fire me. I said, "Go ahead; I am not going to stop our progress because of jealousy." The Tal Afar city council took the position that they had voted me in, and the Nineveh provincial council did not have the authority to fire me.

When the citizens of Tal Afar learned about the threat to fire me, they—Shi'a and Sunni alike—demonstrated peacefully, hoisting me to their shoulders and carrying me through the streets, chanting that they would not let me go.

To this day, I believe the best part of our work together was that LTC Hickey, Col. McMaster, and I were able to bring rival factions together under one umbrella.

The (Rocky) Way Ahead

When Iraq was voting for a new constitution, the Diyala Governate, the city of Mosul, the Kurdish people, and Shi'a Muslims voted for the constitution. During the voting, the governor called me from Mosul to ask how the turnout looked for the vote.

I said "I only see Shi'a."

He said, "Everyone in Baghdad is waiting to see how Tal Afar votes to know whether the referendum will pass."

Now people complain that the constitution is bad, that it is too much influenced by the American Constitution. I think the Sunni made a serious miscalculation. The Sunni were discouraged from voting or participating in government in any way. Now though, if we want to change it, the Kurds, with three provinces, could prevent it.

14   Christopher Hickey Interview

"They did not sever his head, but they cut him open and filled him with explosives so that when his father tried to retrieve his body, they both exploded."

I was doing a leader's reconnaissance in the "Triangle of Death" south of Baghdad when Colonel [later retired LTG Herbert R.] McMaster came to headquarters and said that I would be going to Tal Afar instead.

When I arrived in Tal Afar in early in April 2005, the squadron commander who was in charge brought me up to speed about the situation in Tal Afar. I took over as commander on 1 May 2005.

Najim al Jubouri had just been named chief of police. There was a new Iraqi brigade commander and I was the new American commander, so all three of the city's leaders were new and unfamiliar with the city. We were all outsiders, and the fact that we were all overwhelmed probably helped us to bond. We knew that we had much work to do together.

When I arrived in Tal Afar, I quickly got in contact with the platoon and troop level troops in Sarai, the oldest Sunni section of the city. The American Armored Cavalry unit was partnered with Iraqi battalions to patrol throughout the city. In addition to the city itself, we knew that the insurgents cached their weapons in a forest just to the south.

Tal Afar was a gunfight. When I first met him, Najim was wearing a blue uniform shirt with his military rank. In typical Arab fashion, we started out talking about our families and sharing pictures. As this was my second deployment to Iraq—I had previously been deployed to Fallujah, so I knew what it was to be in a real gun fight—I was familiar with the Arab custom of discussing family and drinking tea before getting down to business. It was another aspect of our burgeoning relationship that helped us to bond quickly with each other.

At first we spent a lot of time, maybe 30-60 days, just trying to figure out who had the power and who was where. I knew it wasn't about good guys and bad guys. It was never that clear.

What we figured out right away was that the Shi'a were not interested in fighting us, and going on the offensive against the 70% of the city that were Sunni didn't seem sensible. We didn't want to be seen as pro-Shi'a; we wanted to be seen on the side of the Iraqi government.

The previous mayor was Shi'a, and it appeared that he used the Shi'ite police force as a hit squad.

For reasons of safety and security, Najim and I started meeting with people only in the director's office at the hospital. When we met with Sunni sheikhs, formally or informally, we just listened. Of course, we spent hours and hours talking about family and drinking tea and soda.

One of my first and enduring contacts was Sheikh Wali, a chicken farmer and a feisty leader interested only in protecting his people and going after Sunni. He always treated us with respect but got frustrated when we went to talk with the Sunni in their areas. I tried to help him understand that we couldn't stabilize the city only by talking to Shi'a.

Before long we had started to detect disparate parts of the insurgency, not just "us against them." Some of them were former Ba'athists who were angry and resentful because we had kicked them out of power and elected educated people. Some of the sheikhs were highly educated people, mostly secular. Some of them were former jet pilots. It was more about no longer being in power than it was about us. We thought we could reason with some of them, bring them into the system we were trying to establish in Tal Afar.

Not surprisingly, radical Islamist groups who wanted to kill us would not meet with us. They were part of (Abu Musab) al Zarqawi's network, pretty ruthless. They would cut off heads and leave bodies in the street with the severed heads left on top of the bodies and IEDs under them. It was only about 5% of the population, but they had assassination squads to capture and kill anyone they saw as the enemy.

Maybe the worst case I saw was that of a young boy who was killed. They did not sever his head, but they cut him open and filled him with explosives so that when his father tried to retrieve his body, they both exploded.

I started mapping out the power structure: Who was who; who was associated with whom; how did they relate to each other? We talked to the Turkmen Front, a political party, and the Sunni political party who had a couple of positions in Tal Afar. We thought their supporters were part of the insurgency.

When it was safe, we could go to their headquarters to listen to their grievances. They had some serious misconceptions about us, about our intentions and mission, and they had some legitimate grievances

One of the first meetings in the hospital was with a fighter pilot, a Sunni sheikh who saw me as an opposing force guy. I said, "I am here to establish conditions for safe elections. Tal Afar is 70% Sunni. We want to allow everyone to register to vote," I said, "Doesn't that bode well for you?"

It was easy to see what had to happen. We had fewer than 100 police officers, most of them Shi'a and all of them afraid to leave the castle. To gain trust, we needed to recruit a police force that mirrored the population. We had to grow the police force by five or six hundred officers.

We met with Sunni and Shi'ite sheikhs to recruit for the police. We mainly used troops, both U.S. and Iraqi, to recruit. We were getting frustrated that Sunni leaders said "We support you," and they promised to recruit for the police but nobody showed. And that happened over and over.

Because of the fear that people felt in talking with us, we arranged to meet in secret at the old fort, 5-10 kilometers (3-6 miles) east of the city. The castle was a big rectangle with white walls. It must have been over a hundred years old.

One Sunni sheikh who had just been released from prison in Baghdad where he had been held as part of the insurgency, joined us. I asked why Sunnis were not joining the police force. He said, "We have a radical Islamic group in our neighborhood. If I or my sons or daughters join you, they will kill us and our families."

I said tell us where we can find them.

He said, "I can't. They'll kill us."

In early June, some cooperating Sunnis provided intelligence that made it possible for me to take the squadron in and capture 26 to 30 of them.

The Sunni waited for a reaction. They knew their weakness was informants. So then we went to clean up a Shi'a neighborhood. We told them, "You have 24 hours to go, or you are dead." The only danger in Shi'a neighborhoods, was mortar attacks from their Sunni neighbors. But we had mortar-detecting radar, and we could shoot Paladins at the mortars and take them out of action in a fraction of a second. So the mortar attacks were very brief and then the men and their mortars would have to change to another location. We had air cover from helicopters, so we could see if friendlies were working in the area. Otherwise, Shi'a neighborhoods were safe; they had their own militia. The mixed neighborhoods were very dangerous. We knew if we entered Sunni neighborhoods we would take fire: gunfire, machine-guns, IEDs, etc.

In July we began getting pressure from Baghdad to resolve the situation in Tal Afar. I believe the pressure on Baghdad came from the Shi'ite neighborhood, and Baghdad applied the pressure to Najim and me.

Later that month, Sunni leaders went to Baghdad for a peace conference along with a former mayor. The former mayor was Sunni, and he had a separate city hall in a Sunni neighborhood where he could safely stay in the northeast sector instead of in the real city hall in the castle. And that's another reason that we knew he was part of the insurgency.

When the Sunni sheikhs returned from Baghdad the city was quiet. There was no gunfire from machine guns. There were no more mortars. So we met at the hospital to hear the result of the meetings in Baghdad. The Sunni sheikhs said, "Look, the peace conference was a success. There is no fighting in Tal Afar; it has become quiet."

They were right. In 24 hours Tal Afar had gone from Dodge City to total quiet. But to us that showed only that the insurgency was centralized and that the sheikhs had control over it, not that the peace conference was a success.

By that time Fallujah had become a synonym for a war zone, as in "You're not going to Fallujah us!" The sheikhs argued that, since the streets in the city were calm, there was no need for a military operation. Calm had descended on the city. Clearly, the peace conference was intended as a deterrent, a preemptive strike against a major military operation in the city. Strategically, that made perfect sense. Between Syria and Baghdad, Tal Afar was the center for insurgent planning and for storing weapons and supplies. When the city was calm the insurgents could work under the radar. We understood that the "peace" was a ploy.

The first thing we did was to build a berm about 12 meters high, 8 feet, that encircled the city. It took my unit a month with heavy equipment to complete the berm. We left five roads to enter or leave the city, and we set up checkpoints at each of these roads to check identification and to search for contraband. Of course the checkpoints were dangerous because of the possibility of car bombs.

At the same time, we patrolled the area with helicopters and UAVs (Unmanned Aerial Vehicles, or drones). That would have been August 2005. We also started doing reconnaissance in the surrounding villages to monitor the power structure.

Meanwhile the Iraqi Army was getting better and better. It was like introducing the Army to its own people. The Iraqi Army was certain that all Tal Afar citizens were terrorists. The Iraqi troops were green, uninitiated troops, from the enlisted men up to the captain. Even those who were Sunni were secular Sunni who were holdovers from the older Army, well-trained and intelligent. Their loyalty was to Iraq not to a sect. The Iraqi Army was probably the strongest institution in Iraq. The field grade officers were the best.

When they arrived in Tal Afar, the young troops sprayed death blossoms [rapid, scattered fire in all directions] every time they were startled. They were a danger to their fellow soldiers and to the citizens.

The Iraqi Army tried to copy us, the American forces. It was like emulating NFL players. They learned once fired upon to get down and take cover, focus on the origin of the fire, and to hold their own fire until they could clearly identify the target.

Over the telephone, an American general, Lieutenant General John Vines from the U.S. Army's XVIII Airborne Corps and Multinational Corps, had broad but specific guidance. He said, "It does me no good if your ops are American-centered. We need the Iraqis to take charge. We need to work ourselves out of a job and get the Iraqis to run ops for themselves."

The good thing about having a lot of Iraqis with us was that, as an armored cavalry unit, we were not accustomed to doing operations dismounted. The Iraqi Army provided the dismount capability to complement our own capabilities. We had at least one interpreter with each platoon.

We worked hard at being non-threatening. Whenever I met with Iraqis, I made sure to take my gear off first: vest, helmet, sunglasses, everything intimidating, so that I could connect with the people as people.

I learned how I acted could make people want to not fight us, and teaching my men to do the same was a force multiplier.

I'd say 90% of the people just wanted to raise their families, and to live out their lives in peace.

By August, pressure from Baghdad was mounting. We had orders to do a major op, so we started planning. We needed more than I had. Operation Restoring Rights started September 2005. We had a cavalry squadron to reinforce us. The 82nd Airborne Unit 325, our sister unit, took the east side of the city; we took the west. A tactical squadron reinforced Unit 325. Our own reinforcements were heavily Kurdish. They had a special forces A-Team (special operators), which headquartered with us. I had a B-Team [headquarters detachment].

We had an Iraqi battalion, an American battalion, and a Military Transition Team (MITT) to train headquarters how to run a battalion.

We had checkpoints and police precincts. The A-Team ran tactical operations. They cleared the dangerous Sarai neighborhood and funneled them to a relocation camp we had set up in the South. When we went through to clear the neighborhood, we found that everyone had gone except for a few old people. The Kurds were so rough when they cleared that we sent them back to rejoin their unit. The same was true of the commandos sent from Baghdad.

[LTC, now retired New York congressman] Chris Gibson led the 82nd on the east side, where he had primary responsibility. I had the city from the castle west. I wanted to be sure to maintain the same city-level contacts. It was important for the Iraqis to know and trust their contact. So we tried to keep them consistent. I also knew that it was important to not give the appearance of favoring one side or the other, so if I had a meeting with a Sunni, I'd immediately meet with a Shi'a. They always knew as soon as we met with one group or another.

The people knew that we lived in an abandoned house in the city and, and soon they started coming to tell us where the bad guys were. We were able to coordinate with Iraqi forces, and I moved into the castle where the American forces, Iraqi forces, and Iraqi police were co-located. We had a joint operations center so that we all knew what the others knew and we all knew what the others were doing.

After Operation Restoring Rights [The Battle of Tal Afar], we had Americans living throughout the city, and the bad guys were gone. The Sunni began joining the police force in big numbers. Each time we had about 100 new recruits, we loaded them on C-130s, and sent them to Jordan for training.

Around September 10 or so, we begin bringing all the leaders—U.S. and Iraqi military and Tal Afar police—together every week or 10 days. We had Najim and the new police chief from Mosul—he was a good guy—lived with the Iraqi commander. Najim lived at city hall in the castle. We had such good coordination that if something happened in the city we could just say, "Lock it down," and close down the city. We had four levels of air support.

We kept supplies and fuel at the granary. Missions were now more spontaneous as each smaller unit understood and accepted responsibility for immediate action. The actions and reactions became more organic. Each sector became an organic operation, each supporting the others. Our reactions became so fast that it was too dangerous to be the enemy.

When we arrived in Tal afar, we had felt as if we were the hunted; now we knew that we were the hunters.

Najim always traveled in my Bradley [Fighting Vehicle: BFV]. I said, "Don't you dare go out in anything other than my Bradley because I can't afford to lose you." But sometimes he went to visit schools or police precincts on his own. He took a police car, and, a few times, he was shot at and I'd rip him a new one.

Whenever we went to the schools we left our weapons— body armor, sunglasses, and helmets—outside. Najim would ask students, "Are you Sunni or Shi'a?" No matter which way they answered, Najim would tell them, "I don't like that answer. When someone asks you 'Are you Sunni or Shi'a,' tell them 'I am Iraqi.'"

Then he asked the question again: "Are you Sunni or Shi'a?" and when they answered "Iraqi," he handed out little Iraqi Flags.

And he did not stop with the schools. He would go into a police precinct and ask the officers, "Are you Shi'a or Sunni?" And if they answered either way, he said, "No. You are Iraqi."

We also had checkpoints all around the city with tall banners that gave the impression of the city being under control of the military. They also were a good target for graffiti.

We thought, "Let's pay someone to paint Iraqi flags on them, three foot by three foot Iraqi flags. We found someone, paid him something like $100, and he took his job very seriously. We had Iraqi flags everywhere, and what they said was "The government is in charge again." Their effect was calming.

I most admired my young soldiers who'd survive an IED attack and go out again the next day. I drew my strength from them.

Around maybe January of 2006, our forces had three suspected insurgents in handcuffs lined up against the wall of a house on the north side of the city. We had troops on the roof of that building and the surrounding buildings when an explosive device detonated inside the house where the insurgents were all against the wall. The explosion blew the soldiers off the roof, but they weren't seriously harmed. The only fatalities were the insurgents.

I later learned that when Najim heard that I was at the explosion, he said, "If Colonel Hickey is killed, I will wipe this city out."

We had been a team of teams. When it was time for the 3rd Armored Cav (ACR) to rotate, a new boss came to town, Lieutenant Colonel Tien, a really good man, but Najim seemed depressed. "We worked so well together; we accomplished so much together; and now you are leaving," Najim said. "I'm quitting."

Iraqis have long memories. When I was there they talked glowingly about Lieutenant Colonel [Gregory] Pace who served under General Petraeus. He was always remembered as a good guy, even by Sunni guys I had pretty much concluded were insurgents. I was trying to do the best I could for the leaders and for the city. All night long I would get calls from both sides to mediate their disagreements.

Ramadan came in late October/early November that year, and Najim and I were invited to a different iftar [the evening meal to break the fast at sunset] every night. I'd get out of my gear and we'd go to a different private home almost every night. Of course the meal has religious significance but I also sensed that people brought us into their homes out of gratitude for what we have accomplished in Tal Afar.

~~~~~

On Christmas Day, a bunch of Shi'ite and Sunni leaders came to the castle. They said, "We have a present for you."

It was a Christmas tree. And they also had big cakes and sodas. Pepsis, I remember. They said, "We wish you a very happy Christmas."

My birthday is on December of 31, New Year's Eve. I was very touched when the sheikhs presented me with a birthday cake. It said, "Happy Birthday Heky."

But it was the thought--and it really counted.

15   War and Politics

"Al-Qaeda made my assassination a priority, and their attempts grew more organized and aggressive."

Losing the 3rd Armored Cavalry

LTC Hickey and Col. H. R. McMaster were my close and trusted allies. Together we made a formidable team and we were making a clear, positive change in Tal Afar. I was stunned in 2006, when they told me that their time in Tal Afar was over. They were being rotated home.

Our time together had gone by quickly, as it does when one works closely with people he likes and trusts. In this case it was about eight months. I was completely taken by surprise and very saddened. They had become my friends as much as close allies; I had forgotten that they were soldiers in a war zone who would be returning home.

The night that I learned they were leaving Tal Afar, I lay awake, thinking about the ramifications of their leaving. I thought about how we had used our time together, how we had started something really good in Tal Afar. The team I had relied on so heavily, the team that had provided solid and unwavering support, was breaking up. As dawn approached, I decided to write a letter to General [George] Casey [then senior coalition commander in Iraq] and President [George W.] Bush.

I took out a pen and some paper and began to write. It was not intended to be for publication or posterity. It was a simple letter that I wrote in one draft and that a sergeant named Lumley translated into English, with assistance from Major Sean McLaughlin.

I understand that Sgt Lumley has preserved my original

Craig Lancto

handwritten letter.

I am honored that the Third Cavalry Museum at Fort Hood, Texas, displays a handsome facsimile of it. I had no thought that my letter would assume something of an historic status.

~~~~~~

My Letter to America

Feb 16, 2006
From: Mayor of Tall 'Afar, Ninewah, Iraq
In the Name of God the Compassionate and Merciful

To the Courageous Men and Women of the 3d Armored Cavalry Regiment, who have changed the city of Tall' Afar from a ghost town, in which terrorists spread death and destruction, to a secure city flourishing with life. To the lion-hearts who liberated our city from the grasp of terrorists who were beheading men, women and children in the streets for many months.

To those who spread smiles on the faces of our children, and gave us restored hope, through their personal sacrifice and brave fighting, and gave new life to the city after hopelessness darkened our days, and stole our confidence in our ability to reestablish our city.

Our city was the main base of operations for Abu Mousab Al Zarqawi. The city was completely held hostage in the hands of his henchmen. Our schools, governmental services, businesses and offices were closed. Our streets were silent, and no one dared to walk them. Our people were barricaded in their homes out of fear; death awaited them around every corner. Terrorists occupied and controlled the only hospital in the city. Their savagery reached such a level that they stuffed the corpses of children with explosives and tossed them into the streets in order to kill grieving parents attempting to retrieve the bodies of their young. This was the situation of our city until God prepared and delivered unto them the courageous soldiers of the 3d Armored Cavalry Regiment, who liberated this city, ridding it of Zarqawi's followers after harsh fighting, killing many terrorists, and forcing the remaining butchers to flee the city like rats to the surrounding

105

areas, where the bravery of other 3d ACR soldiers in Sinjar, Rabiah, Zumar and Avgani finally destroyed them.

I have met many soldiers of the 3d Armored Cavalry Regiment; they are not only courageous men and women, but avenging angels sent by The God Himself to fight the evil of terrorism.

The leaders of this Regiment; COL McMaster, COL Armstrong, LTC Hickey, LTC Gibson, and LTC Reilly embody courage, strength, vision and wisdom.

Officers and soldiers alike bristle with the confidence and character of knights in a bygone era.

The mission they have accomplished, by means of a unique military operation, stands among the finest military feats to date in Operation Iraqi Freedom, and truly deserves to be studied in military science. This military operation was clean, with little collateral damage, despite the ferocity of the enemy. With the skill and precision of surgeons they dealt with the terrorist cancers in the city without causing unnecessary damage.

God bless this brave Regiment; God bless the families who dedicated these brave men and women. From the bottom of our hearts we thank the families. They have given us something we will never forget. To the families of those who have given their holy blood for our land, we all bow to you in reverence and to the souls of your loved ones. Their sacrifice was not in vain. They are not dead, but alive, and their souls hovering around us every second of every minute. They will never be forgotten for giving their precious lives. They have sacrificed that which is most valuable. We see them in the smile of every child, and in every flower growing in this land. Let America, their families, and the world be proud of their sacrifice for humanity and life.

Finally, no matter how much I write or speak about this brave Regiment, I haven't the words to describe the courage of its officers and soldiers. I pray to God to grant happiness and health to these legendary heroes and their brave families.

NAJIM ABDULLAH ABID AL-JIBOURI
Mayor of Tall 'Afar,
Ninewah, Iraq

~~~~~~

Craig Lancto

America Responds

The first reaction to the letter came from General Casey, It was a genuine and human response to the loss I had described at the 3d Armored Cavalry Regiment's withdrawal from Nineveh.

In his letter, General Casey reminded me that the soldiers have family too, that they had done their duty and deserved to see their loved ones. And he promised me that he would choose a unit at least equal to the 3rd ACR, with a commander at least as good as Colonel McMaster, and a regiment commander who is the equal of LTC Hickey.

With the arrival of Colonel [later Major General] Sean McFarland and LTC John Tien[4], General Casey fulfilled his promise. In fact, when Colonel McFarland was later transferred to Ramadi, in the Anbar Governate, the seat of resistance against U.S. Forces in Iraq from 2003-2006, he carried the lessons from Tal Afar and initiated what would be known as the *Anbar Awakening*.

The loss of Col. McMaster and LTC Hickey was great. They were not only trusted allies, but they were dear and valued friends.

If each of them was weighed against an equal weight of gold, they would prove the more valuable. I have not said much about Colonel McMaster's deputy, Colonel Joel Armstrong, but I must add that he also was a trusted and valued friend and a gallant soldier.

Not long after my letter was delivered, Colonel McMaster called me to say that I should watch President Bush's speech on March 10. He didn't tell me why, only that I should listen carefully.

Over the next few days, he called several times to remind me to watch the president's speech. He also sent another officer to be sure that I watched the speech. I was very curious, but never expected what actually happened.

Colonel Mahmoud, my deputy police chief, and I watched the president's speech on "The War on Terror and Operation Iraqi Freedom" in my office[5]. At the time, my English was very poor, but

[4]   Col. Tien (ret.), managing director of Citigroup, was a Rhodes scholar. He has served as senior national security advisor to both President Obama and President Bush.

107

major speeches were subtitled in Arabic.

It was George W. Bush, the president of the United States talking about the unpopularity of U.S. military operations in Iraq. He talked about how often the U.S. had been criticized for mistakes in Iraq, and then he began talking about a successful operation; he talked about Tal Afar, a safe haven and refuge for insurgents, a hive of terrorist activity slightly more than 35 miles from the Syrian border. He cited the horrors of terrorists, such as kidnapping a sick child, planting explosives inside of him, and leaving him where his family would find him so that their child would explode and kill or maim them. He talked about al-Qaeda's reign of terror and destruction in Tal Afar, and then he talked about what we had done about it. He talked about the important role of the 3d ACR and how they had worked closely with me and my security forces to rid the city of terror.

And then, the President of the United States read excerpts from my letter to General Casey. I understood why Col. McMaster had urged me to watch the speech.

For an American, being singled out by the President of the United States is a unique honor, an honor shared by a handful every year. For a simple Iraqi soldier who had only answered the call of duty as police chief in a lawless town, as mayor of a city in decline, as an ally who worked closely with American soldiers to repair the damage of Saddam Hussein, al-Qaeda and years of neglect and mistrust, it was an undreamed honor.

He detailed successes in Tal Afar, success that I had planned with the strong support of my American friends. He mentioned the role of Colonel McMaster in the hard work to resuscitate a dying city. He said, let America be proud to have an ally such as the mayor of Tal Afar...to be proud of me.

I was stunned.

The Greeks would say, "Let me die now." This honor was as great as any I might hope for in my life and I was profoundly moved by the president's words.

---

5   Excerpts from the speech follow the Foreword to this book.

I was proud that I had been part of a program that brought honor to the American forces and my adopted city. I was proud that the president of the United States, the most powerful country in the world, reserved a few words of praise for me. After the trials I had faced in Iraq, this felt like vindication. It was more reward than I could have hoped for.

In Tal Afar, the reaction to the president's speech generally was pride and a redoubled faith in me, my administration, and the American forces who had proven to be good and faithful friends. In the minds of the residents, having the president of the United States commend their mayor was proof of their wisdom and foresight in having me as their top local government official. It was proof that I was not like all the other mayors in Iraq, that I had made a difference in their lives.

As a result, I found new and stronger support for the work of my administration. I became more effective because I had won their unconditional confidence. People were more willing to work with me. The U.S. forces in Nineveh had greater trust because their president had singled me out.

I believe that the quality of America's military leaders is uniformly high, but the 3rd Armored Cavalry Division seemed to enjoy an unusual number of exceptional leaders. Working with these brave and noble men was more than any soldier could reasonably hope for.

Before Colonel McMaster rotated out, he told me that there would be a ceremony in the United States to honor the brave men who had fallen in Tal Afar. I told him that I wanted to be there.

On May 19, 2006, I was in Colorado Springs to attend a 3d Armored Cavalry ceremony to honor those who had given their lives in Iraq. I brought with me letters from sheikhs, both Sunni and Shi'a, entreating the United States not to withdraw troops from Iraq. I was especially honored that they made me an honorary citizen of Colorado Springs at that ceremony.

A few days later, a blogger named Frank Warner reported on my comments, through an interpreter because I still had almost no English:

"Are you truly my friends?" he asked through a translator. "Yes. I walk a happier man because you are my friends. You are the world to me. I smell the sweet perfume that emanates from the flower of your strength, honor and greatness in every corner of Tal Afar. The nightmares of terror fled when the lion of your bravery entered our city."

"One year ago today, not even a bird used to be inside the city of Tal Afar because of all the shooting that happened continuously," he said. "All of the schools were closed and all the government facilities were closed completely. Killing and murdering was allowed—even of the children."

Mr. Warner reported that the mayor said just two words in English at that welcome-home ceremony: "Thank you."

According to *The Rocky Mountain News*, he added, those two words brought a standing ovation.

The Americans don't liberate nations for a thank you, he concluded. They liberate nations because it is the duty of free people to free the oppressed wherever they can, and because a freer world is a better, more peaceful world.

But a thank you is so polite.

Since the 3rd Armored Cavalry left Tal Afar, I am happy to report that Colonel McMaster and I have remained close friends with frequent contact.

Iraqi Backlash to the President's Speech

But there was a downside to the publicity surrounding my letter and the president's mentioning me in his speech. As if to prove the truth of Christ's words that a prophet is without honor in his home town, I faced jealousy and personal attacks. This was, after all, Iraq, where jealousy and factionalism and sectarianism are woven into the ancient fabric of society. Praise for me was considered tacit criticism of all the other mayors in the country. My city's success meant that others were failures. My public commendation for vanquishing al-Qaeda was a challenge to the terrorists for revenge. And al-Qaeda and their supporters throughout the country were incited to destroy me and to reverse the progress we had made in my city.

110

Al-Qaeda made my assassination a priority, and their attempts grew more organized and aggressive.

In the summer of 2007, they found my house in Mosul, filled it with explosives and destroyed it completely. Thankfully, U.S. forces have a close relationship with the government of the autonomous region of Kurdistan and as a result of assassination threats, in 2005, they had arranged with the Kurdish government for my family to live in Dohuk, Kurdistan. Ordinarily, Arabs are prohibited from settling in Kurdish territory, but because al-Qaeda was intent on killing my family and me, they made an exception. In fact, my parents had lived in Kurdistan from about 1975-1985 because of my father's work as a national policeman when I was in school in Baghdad.

Kurdish security forces, a particularly competent and professional force, warned us that they were receiving reports that al-Qaeda was actively looking for my family in Kurdistan.

Col. McFarland and the 1st Armored Division in Tal Afar

The 1st Armored Division ("Old Ironsides") was the unit replacing the 3d ACR. Col. Sean McFarland was brigade commander, LTC John Tien was regimental commander, the roles previously filled by Col McMaster and LTC Hickey, respectively.

I was pleased to see that they clearly were both well-briefed on the situation in Tal Afar, and more pleased that Col. McFarland talked with me for long hours, eager to learn about Iraq and Iraqi culture, an encouraging portent.

Col. McFarland knew that Col. McMaster had enjoyed unprecedented success in Tal Afar and he aspired to replicate it. I suspect that he also had been told how distressed I was when Col. McMaster and LTC Hickey left, and that it was important to reassure me and the people of Tal Afar that nothing had changed, that Col. McFarland was up to the task and that Tal Afar remained in good hands.

One officer from the 3d ACR, Cpt. (FNU) Marimoto, requested and was granted an extension and stayed with me at the castle after the transition. The 1st Armored Division, Headquarters Brigade, stayed at Tal Afar Airport, and troops remained stationed at outposts throughout the city.

With the 1st Armored Division, we moved ahead with projects in

Tal Afar. We dug wells for people who had no access to potable water, paved streets that were unfit for vehicles, and built schools to prepare for the future of Tal Afar.

Perhaps more important, we continued meeting with the city council and the sheikhs who served on the Brotherly Dialogue Committee to encourage reconciliation.

It seemed that almost every day saw an opening ceremony for another of the myriad renewal projects in the city, and American generals, including General Martin Dempsey, who would become chairman of the Joint Chiefs of Staff, continually came to Tal Afar to see firsthand what we were accomplishing.

16   A New Crisis

"The trouble was how to resolve a serious conflict in which both parties believe that they have been wronged."

When I was finally able to get away for a rare visit with my family in Dohuk, I received urgent calls from the city council and the council of sheikhs They said that I had to return as quickly as possible, the city was ready to ignite and everything we had achieved was about to be destroyed.

A Perilous Arrest

I rushed back to Tal Afar—fortunately, I had a police car which significantly reduced the time—to find the city in an uproar. American forces had arrested two Sunni women for terrorism, and they were holding them at the airport. As troops searched the city, the women had vowed that no one was in their respective homes. When troops found men with hand grenades hiding in their closets, the women were arrested.

It is difficult for Americans to appreciate the significance of those arrests. I think many Americans are aware that in Arab culture—especially in Muslim culture—men and women are often treated differently. In mosques, women are separated from men. In strictly observant countries such as Saudi Arabia, restaurants have separate seating for women or families with women, so that other patrons will not see the women unveiled. Some public businesses—as mundane as a shawarma shop—prohibit women.

Modesty is paramount. Even when women are not "covered," that is dressed in burqas and veils, they often keep their hair covered. They are not permitted to be alone with a male who is not related to them by blood or marriage. They do not go out unaccompanied. In some countries a woman who commits adultery is sentenced to death. I suspect that most Americans have heard of "honor killings," in which families kill their own daughter or sister who has so much as been alone with a male who is not related. Men do not generally ask about the women in another man's family, and the women often remain in a different room while the men talk. As in any religion—as with any tradition—the range of behaviors is broad. But two foreign soldiers—most likely not Muslims—had taken two unchaperoned women into their custody. At very least, this experience was a shame upon the women, their respective families, and Islam.

Iraq itself has a range of levels of religious strictness. But in Muslim culture, no matter how observant, two women being taken away by male American soldiers dishonors the women and their families. That they were taken and were being held by non-Muslims was a powder keg, almost literally. To Shi'a and Sunni alike, it was an outrage. American troops who did not understand the culture were not likely to realize what an egregious act arresting the women was. They saw a criminal act and arrested the perpetrators without regard to—or ignorant of—religious or cultural sensitivities. The Americans were acting justly when they made the arrests. The city's Muslims were acting justly, being true to their faith, when they deplored the act which violated rules the Americans didn't understand.

The trouble was how to resolve a serious conflict in which both parties believe that they have been wronged. The women had been apprehended committing a crime. The soldiers had unwittingly violated Sharia law.

It was genuinely a crisis.

The media in Mosul, and as far as Baghdad, had harsh words for the arrest of the two women, which became a major scandal.

The city was tense. Crowds were gathering in the streets.

I arrived in my office to find the city council and a number of sheikhs, both Sunni and Shi'a, all talking at once. "This is wrong!" They said. "This is an outrage! This is a disaster!"

Crisis Averted

I sent LTC Tien to the airport to arrange an urgent meeting with Colonel McFarland. As soon as it was arranged, I left to meet with him.

When I explained how grave the situation was, Col. McFarland protested that the women had been caught in the act. They were terrorists.

I asked, "How many terrorists do you think there are in Tal Afar? 200-300?"

He guessed around 300.

I asked, "Do you think that it will be the end of the U.S. Army if there are 302? Women's honor is sacred here; this incident will have repercussions not only in Tal Afar, but across Iraq. *Al Jazeera* will exploit it and anger will spread, but if we use it the right way, we can turn the situation to our advantage."

"I suggest that we release them on their sheikh's personal guarantee that they will speak to other women about the consequences of participating in terrorist acts. Doing so burnishes my image as mayor [in successfully arguing for their release] as well as the image of the U.S. troops who appear chivalrous and respectful and wanting to the right thing."

"We take the public relations weapon of our destruction out of the hands of the media and the insurgents and turn it to our advantage as the women go about the business of dissuading others from helping the terrorists and of persuading them that the U.S. forces are the good guys. The pros greatly outweigh the cons."

Col. McFarland paused briefly before nodding. "Okay," he said.

So we called for some Sunni sheikhs to come to the castle, where they signed personal guarantees for the women, and we released them to the sheikhs The protest demonstrations in the street became great celebrations, and I was able to try again to visit my family. But, as I left the city, my car was repeatedly stopped by people celebrating in the streets, and they cheered and shook my hand and thanked me for the women's release.

Ramadi, The Turning Point

After four or five months working together, the 1st Armored Division, Headquarters Brigade, was transferred to Ramadi—sometimes called al-Qaeda's capital city—in Anbar Province. Soon after settling in, they sent the mayor of Ramadi to stay with me in Tal Afar so that he could see how we were bringing about change. And that is how the strategies and techniques that transformed Tal Afar became the seed of the movement known as the Battle of Ramadi (June through November of 2006) and the Anbar Awakening that arose from it when a Sunni sheikhs banded together to drive insurgents out of the city.

In some ways it was easier in Ramadi. The capital of Anbar Province is a Sunni city, so they did not have to deal with the vehement and overt sectarianism that faced Tal Afar, but they did face insurgents holding the hospital and the government center, and they followed our lead in establishing combat operating posts in which American and Iraqi troops were deployed throughout the city.

Also, following the model of Tal Afar and al Basra, U.S. forces cordoned off neighborhoods, cleared the houses and conducted house-to-house searches for weapons and terrorists. They used surgical airstrikes, controlled the roads to cut off the flow of explosives and weapons, exchanged fire with insurgents, and retook the city.

In September, insurgents in Ramadi killed a sheikh who was encouraging the men in his tribe to join the local police, and they denied him proper burial. That was the precipitating incident for about forty Sunni sheikhs to band together to drive the insurgents out of Ramadi in what has become known as the Anbar Awakening, which signaled the death of al-Qaeda in Iraq.

After the Battle

At the end of 2006/beginning of 2007, the United States began drawing down troops in Iraq. Instead of a division (three brigades), a single brigade (3,000-5,000 soldiers) under the command of Colonel Malcolm Frost was assigned to Tal Afar. Colonel Frost lived at the airport and withdrew all U.S. troops from the Combat Operating Posts throughout the city. Iraqi police and military continued to occupy them.

America reduced aid for rebuilding the city and left the responsibility to the central Iraqi government, under whom the projects were poorly managed.

While Tal Afar was regularly featured on television, and throughout Iraq, the citizens and leaders of other towns and cities patiently awaited their turn at reconstruction. They were confident that the public works modernizing Tal Afar would also come to their respective municipalities.

I told the American leadership that I could not rely on support from the government, local or national. For one thing, rather than taking pride in our accomplishments in Tal Afar, the central government, cueing on grumblings from other towns and cities, resented the rebirth of Tal Afar and the national attention it attracted.

The central government launched an effort to remove me as mayor. They renewed charges that I—and other military leaders from the old army—were unreformed Ba'athists. Well, we had been Ba'athists—members of a state party dedicated to the renaissance of Arab culture, values, and society—but under Saddam, being a military officer required being a member of the Ba'ath party.

People in the central government petitioned Mosul's governor and the chief of provincial police who recruited me to fire me. Obviously, I could not rely on that central government to support my efforts to continue the work of rebuilding Tal Afar.

I begged the American forces not to abandon us before the work was done. I talked with colonels Twitty and Frost and every general who came to see what we were doing in Tal Afar. The answer always was the same: We can't stay.

In 2007, some American officers came to the castle and said that they wanted me to come with them to the U.S. forces' headquarters at the Tal Afar airport. When I arrived at the airport I was surprised to see General David Petraeus, then commander of Coalition Forces in Iraq; Mufk al Rbui, the Iraqi Minister of Security; and Idn Khalid, Deputy Minister of the Interior there.

General Petraeus said, "Look, Mayor, I have brought representatives from the central Iraqi government to talk with you about how to complete the mission you have begun with the U.S.

forces in Tal Afar."

I said, "You know what Tal Afar was like before we started. You saw the deteriorated infrastructure, the crumbling buildings, and the roads so ruined that they were almost completely unusable. The city was in better condition 1,000 or 2,000 years ago than it was when we started rebuilding."

"If we don't finish the job, it is a victory for al-Qaeda. They will return in force."

The Minister of Security said, "We can't do this. We can't do that."

The Deputy Minister of the Interior said, "You can't let them come back. Tal Afar needs—deserves—our support."

The Minister of Security said, "We can't do it."

General Petraeus was clearly becoming frustrated. He said, "Okay, we will keep some U.S. forces in Tal Afar to complete the work that we started together."

And, true to General Petraeus's word, U.S. forces remained in Tal Afar and the U.S. continued to support our efforts to rebuild the city. It was a partnership unmatched by any other city in Iraq.

A Bloody Message

But al-Qaeda was not ready to surrender the city. They continued to sow discord and discontent. They exploded car bombs and suicide bombs and kept the city off balance and on alert. They created almost insuperable problems for us because once one person is killed, his family must retaliate and his neighbors spur them on to revenge. When a Shi'ite is killed, a Sunni must die and vice versa. It is a cycle without end.

U.S. officers and I talked with the people of Tal Afar in an effort to reduces tension and calm tempers.

In March 2007, a large truck with five or six tons of explosives was set off near a Shi'a area. Some Sunni families also were affected. The massive explosion left, I think, 10 dead and about 30 injured.

Some Shi'a police killed about 50 Sunni in retaliation. We charged them with dereliction of duty including the deputy commander of an

Iraqi brigade. I ordered him out of the area and fired many of our Shi'a police officers. Many Shi'a came to me and said, "Mayor, please do something. We can feel that something bad is coming."

This was the worst incident since the Battle of Tal Afar and we thought that we were seeing the beginning of the destruction of everything that we had worked for.

We held talks with sheikhs from both sects. Shi'as held major demonstrations in the streets, protesting the firing of nearly a dozen Shi'a police officers.

At last all parties agreed to settle the matters in court.

Colonel Twitty remained very actively involved. Although he lived in Mosul, he made frequent visits to Tal Afar. He continued being a great support to me, and when the roads were blocked with rubble and crowds, he saved many lives by using American helicopters to transport the injured to U.S. hospitals in Mosul.

A Grateful Population

The citizens of Tal Afar were reassured that the Americans had not deserted us when they saw the helicopters sweeping into the rescue. They knew that the American forces were still watching over Tal Afar.

Countless citizens said "God bless you," when they saw me. I said, "Not me; ask God to bless Colonel Twitty and the American forces."

I sensed that Colonel [now, LTG, Stephen] Twitty was ill at the time, but he recovered and I believe that the blessings and prayers of so many of the citizens of Tal Afar brought about the remission. Nevertheless, I don't think that anyone understood and appreciated how much Col. Twitty did for Tal Afar.

LTC [now Major General, Malcolm] Frost also did much to improve relations with the people of Tal Afar. The people and I felt very close to him.

An American journalist writing for one of the military publications came to Tal Afar. As we stood with Col. Frost looking out over the city, the journalist noted my repeated references to Col. McMaster and LTC Hickey. He asked whether I now consider Col Frost my friend. I sensed that Col. Frost tensed at the awkward question. He was, after all, standing right next to us.

I said, ""No, he is not my friend."

Col. Frost appeared to deflate, however slightly, until I completed the thought: "He is my brother." I was pleased to learn that General Petraeus noted the comment and expressed his pleasure at it to Col. Frost.

Beginning in 2008, before Col. Frost left, Gen [Kevin J.] Brigner [former Deputy Commanding General for Multinational Forces in Mosul] came to see Col. McMaster.

We talked about Tal Afar—We had been friends for a long time. He had been with us in Mosul, although now with the Coalition forces in Baghdad—and I told him how greatly American forces have changed Tal Afar.

He asked how.

I said this time?

He said yes.

If you trust me, take my hand and walk through this neighborhood with Col. McMaster and me.

We walked through the neighborhood and talked with many of the people we met in both Shi'a and Sunni neighborhoods. The people were very happy, especially to see members of American forces walking through their streets unprotected, without even protective vests. They shook hands with us and talked, and he was stunned at the change.

He asked, "What happened here?"

I told him that it was a result of the work of American forces.

But after Col. After Frost left, Tal Afar had only a company at the airbase.

17   Attack on Sinjar

"As we approached Sinjar, I saw what appeared to be huge explosions on the ground."

One day I was returning to Tal Afar from Mosul by helicopter. First we went to Sinjar (also known as Shingar)—on Mount Sinjar on the Syrian border, about 50 km (a little more than 30 miles) south and west of Tal Afar and due west of Mosul—where the United States had an outpost with the Yazidi[6] people.

When I saw what appeared to be huge explosions on the ground near Sinjar, a city of about 88,000 residents, I asked what the American forces were doing, testing nuclear bombs here?

The pilot immediately changed direction and we returned at speed to Tal Afar, where I found an American officer, a major, and asked what had happened.

The major told me that three trucks filled with explosives had been detonated in a village near Sinjar.

I hurried back to the castle and called the hospital director. As Sinjar had only a small clinic and we had experience with bomb victims, I told him to take medical teams to Sinjar without delay.

Then I called General Hashid, but it was Thursday night and, of course, as is often the case in Muslim countries, with the weekend starting on Friday, General Hashid had left early and was not available.

I called Mosul with the same result. The mayor and the director of the clinic in Sinjar called me. They said, "Please help! We have more than 500 injured and we are overwhelmed. We have no beds,

---

[6] An ethnic Kurdish minority indigenous to Iraq, Syria, and Turkey.

no rooms for them. Some are outside awaiting treatment."

I sent all available ambulances and police cars to transport the wounded to the hospital in Tal Afar. Some resisted because they knew Tal Afar only by reputation and feared that it was more dangerous than Sinjar.

I sent out a call to the citizens of Tal Afar to give blood, and we sent more than a hundred of the most seriously wounded to medical facilities in Kurdistan.

There was a large hospital in Mosul, but they told us that they would not accept any of the injured because they feared retaliation from al-Qaeda, who had threatened to kill the drivers and me.

Despite the threats and confusion, we did what we believed was right, and I believe that we did a good job, when the central government and the provincial government wouldn't help.

In the end, we kept about 80 of the injured in the hospital at Tal Afar and dispatched as many doctors as we could spare to Sinjar.

When it was over, the central government in Baghdad reinitiated attempts to fire me. They said that I could no longer control the army and police in Tal Afar. When the people in Tal Afar learned that the central government was trying again to oust me, they took to the streets to demonstrate their opposition.

It was as if every time they remembered Tal Afar—now that it was a safe place to live—the central government renewed efforts to be rid of me. I don't know whether they were embarrassed that Tal Afar had succeeded where most cities had failed or that they feared I was gaining too much power, but they made a concentrated effort to reduce my authority.

After resisting repeated and increasingly assertive efforts to diminish my standing in Tal Afar, I decided that I would leave on my own terms. It was better to leave of my own accord with dignity, to quit while I was strong and I had the solid support of the people of Tal Afar, than to wait for the central government to gradually strip me of my powers and send me away. To my mind, if I stayed, my image—my legacy, as I thought of it—would suffer.

I thought of Zidane, the soccer player, who left Madrid at the top of his game and decided that that was the way I wanted to go out, with

Craig Lancto

dignity, with my head held high. Most important, I would leave Tal Afar far better and stronger than I had found it.

Years later, I still receive frequent telephone calls from leaders of the community, Shi'a and Sunni sheikhs who remember what I had done and tried to do to rebuild the city to its former greatness. They tell me that they look for the day they find another mayor with vision and a firm hand to lead them.

It was a hard four years, one of the lowest points in thousands of years of the city's history, but I was able to be effective because of the forces that came together, U.S. and Iraqi military troops, the police force that I had built from nothing, and Shi'a and Sunni sheikhs all working together to save a once-proud city.

18   An American Perspective

"Al Jubouri is a living legend and positive example of bold leadership...."

U.S. Ambassador Cameron Munter, leader of the first Provincial Reconstruction Team in Nineveh Province from January through July 2006, cabled his perception of Najim to the State Department:(The variant spellings of Arabic names derive from their being transliterations from Arabic script into the Western alphabet.)

22 March 2006

------- SUMMARY -------

Mayor of Tal Afar Najim Al Jubouri -- the hero of President Bush's March 20 speech in Cleveland -- is a rare leader in a country fraught with fear and uncertainty. His strong leadership, both as chief of police and mayor, helped clean up this city of a quarter-million people in northwest Iraq when it was overrun by terrorists and suffering from a decrepit infrastructure. He helped reform the police by making them more representative and accountable. He worked diligently with Coalition Forces and Iraqi Security Forces on counterinsurgency efforts in September 2005. However, he also fears what will become of him and his family once U.S. forces are drawn down in the country. He doubts his countrymen are prepared enough to fully understand democracy, and he questions the sincerity of Iraq's political leadership. He is afraid of sectarian and religious power in Baghdad, and believes that Iran has been behind ethnic tensions in the country. We wonder just how sustainable his efforts in Tal Afar might be once Iraq is left to fend for itself.

-------PROFILE OF A STRONG LEADER-------

Najim Al Jubouri prides himself on being a straight talker and risk taker. He has a history of doing the right thing for his country, often at the expense of his own and his family's personal safety. As chief of police for Tal Afar, Al Jubouri (known simply as "Najim") took an aggressive approach in reforming, training, and equipping the local police to better handle security in the area. His actions did not go unnoticed. An assassination attempt against him was thwarted by a bulletproof vest that proudly hangs on his wall, perhaps as a testament to his convictions or as a reminder of what could have been. Al Jubouri did not walk away from his job, but he did move his family to safety in Baghdad and later to the west Kurdish town of Dohuk. In a city starving for leadership -- especially after its former chief of police, Ismael Faris, fled town leaving in his wake allegations of death and corruption -- Al Jubouri assumed the position of acting mayor in July 2005. 3ACR Commanding Officer, Col H.R. McMaster, instantly identified with Al Jubouri and the two began a partnership that would ultimately benefit the city of Tal Afar. Al Jubouri presided over successful counterinsurgency efforts in September of last year, helping in planning and operations with Coalition and Iraqi Security Forces. That today the dusty little city of Tal Afar has some of the highest levels of available electricity in Iraq and few shortages of potable water is Al Jubouri's work. Al Jubouri is part vigilante, part maverick. He believes he has to work in a system that does not appreciate the struggles of those living outside Iraq's larger cities. He claimed Tal Afar needed strong leadership to battle insurgents that overran it. He found that seeking help from what he saw as a feckless provincial government and a self-absorbed federal government was simply not an option. He said Tal Afar stood in marked contrast to Mosul, since schools were open, kids were playing in the streets, and basic services were met. According to Al Jubouri the central government was now controlled by "sectarians" and "opportunists," and for that reason he adamantly said he would rather report "directly to Washington." He credited the U.S. Army for keeping him alive, for helping to rid Tal Afar of terrorists, and for working to provide everything he needed to run the city.

------MONUMENT TO U.S. INTERVENTION ----
-

Al Jubouri appears to have grown
accustomed to his direct access to CF
[Coalition Forces] and the USG [US
Government]. For this reason he said he
was not preoccupied with issues that
troubled other government officials, such
as providing education, water, and
electricity. Rather, he simply had bigger
ideas for Tal Afar. "I want to construct
a high-rise building like Times Square,"
he said. But if this were not possible a
"large hospital would be nice." As a show
of his respect and admiration for the USG
he claimed his request should not be
misunderstood: he just wanted to build
something that Iraqis could look to as a
monument of the U.S. contribution to the
country. Al Jubouri said he believed the
city of Tal Afar should be made an
example for Iraq with something uniquely
American.

-------SUNNI EXAGGERATIONS ------

When asked about Sunni and Shi'a
relations in the city, Al Jubouri, a
Sunni Arab, said he admitted some Shi'a
Iraqi Police officers were bad. However,
he bitterly accused Sunnis of being
"hypocrites" who "exaggerated" events to

their advantage. He said that when the Golden Mosque in Samarra was bombed on February 22, Shi'as attacked mosques for a few days and then calmed down. He said, however, that if Shi'as had actually bombed an important Sunni shrine, like the Tomb of Abdel Qudir Qadelawi, there would have been "blood on the streets." Al Jubouri accused the predominantly Sunni, Iraqi Islamic Party (IIP), of contributing to tensions between Sunnis and Shi'as. He claimed the IIP did not call for calm after the Samarra bombing, and instead "falsely" announced that three Sunni mosques had been bombed in Tal Afar instead.

------- "KILLER MISTAKES" -------

Although Al Jubouri is clearly a friend of the U.S., he saved his harshest criticism for the USG and its actions in Iraq. "The Americans made a few killer mistakes," he said, and the U.S. "should have never listened" to [deputy prime minister] Ahmed Al Chalabi. They also should not have allowed sectarian Islamic parties to participate in the new government and to help write the constitution, he said. He claimed religious political party involvement in the new constitution had brought Iraq "back hundreds of years." Al Jubouri accused hard-line "religious" parties of being "more dangerous than Saddam Hussein." Since the U.S. was supporting all groups in Iraq, he said, it left the country vulnerable to a sectarian takeover. He claimed "Imams" were dictating politics and "destroying women's rights" by forcing them to "wear tents on their heads." He did not rule out what he claimed was the "strong influence of Iran" that had been contributing to tensions in Iraq. He said the ISF [Iraqi security Forces] was "built incorrectly," since the USG was "training militias" instead of an independent army. As an example he said, "The IA [Iraqi Army] in the north is supported by the Kurds." Lambasting the international media, Al Jubouri called the U.S. press "weak" for not reporting enough on "good stories" in Iraq, especially the work done by CF and the USG. "The U.S. spent a lot of money on schools," said Al Jubouri, "but most Iraqis believe the money came from the Iraqi Government." He claimed Iraqis loved the U.S. but that, too, was "never reported."

------ A FUTURE WITHOUT THE USG ------

"I'll quit," Al Jubouri said immovably when questioned what he would do once CF troops were inevitably drawn down. Al Jubouri said he believed the Iraqi public was not educated enough to understand the profoundly "positive work" that had been done in Tal Afar. He even accused his fellow city council members of being "more interested in helping themselves" than with caring about the city. Al

Jubouri frankly said, "If it was not for
the Coalition Forces we would not have
anything."

------- STILL TIME TO "SAVE IRAQ" ------

Despite his criticisms, Al Jubouri said
he was holding out faith that all was not
yet lost in the country. He suggested
that the USG still had the power to
affect the outcome in Iraq, but that it
would have to act with a "frozen heart."
Al Jubouri recommended that only a
"secularist," like Ayad Allawi, could
lead the country. He said he believed
Allawi was the perfect candidate who
would "work for everyone." "If you fixed
the head, the whole body would be okay.
But right now, things were lopsided," he
claimed. Al Jubouri said democracy was a
foreign concept for Iraqis, and that the
democratic process would take time to
develop. He claimed sectarian parties
took advantage of people's religious and
personal security fears. He said in Basra
before the election, for example, the
Shi'a coalition was marching through the
streets carrying empty caskets, declaring
voters "would die" if they voted for
Allawi. When asked whether the invasion
was worth the effort, Al Jubouri said the
U.S. "won the fight but was losing the
war." He compared the USG to a person
standing in water up to his chest,
looking in panic for a way out. Al
Jubouri said the same tactics that worked
to free Tal Afar from terrorism should

130

also be applied to "liberate Iraq." He recommended the USG install a secular government under Allawi, change the constitution so that it "does not appear like the Koran," and prohibit religious parties from participating. He claimed that these changes would correct the problems in Iraq "within months." He asked that the USG free Iraq the way the Protestant Reformation liberated Europe. He compared life in Iraq and the Middle East today to that of Europe in the 16th and 17th Centuries, where "religious leaders ruled and repressed the people." Once the Europeans were freed, said Al Jubouri, the "whole world changed." And the same could be done for Iraq.

------- COMMENT -------

Najim Al Jubouri is without a doubt a rare and brave leader, and a hero to the people of Tal Afar and Iraq. On a visit to a primary school with the mayor and members of 1/1AD, the students, teachers, and administrators received him with a welcome fit for a king. He firmly believes in "one Iraq," and when he enters a classroom the first question he asks is whether the students are "Sunni or Shi'a" The response, of course, is "We are Iraqis!" Although Al Jubouri is a living legend and positive example of bold leadership in a country fraught with fear and uncertainty, it seems that deep down he is aware that his efforts might be all for naught. This was confirmed when he repeatedly and firmly told us he would "quit" once CF left. We wonder how sustainable his successes will prove if and when the U.S. troops in his area are redeployed.

~~~~~

19 Denouement

"He brought justice to the violent and troubled city of Tal Afar.'

When al-Qaeda targeted Najim and his family family for assassination, H.R. McMaster was instrumental in spiriting them out of Kurdistan and into the United States where he helped them find housing. Also through his agency, Najim was hired by the Near East South Asia Center for Strategic Studies (NESA), one of five regional centers under the auspices of the Department of Defense. At that time, LTG (ret.) David Barno was was the director.

When Najim applied for refugee status, MG McMaster drove from Norfolk, Virginia, to Washington, DC, to attend each hearing in support of his friend.

Despite his many achievements as mayor, police chief, and army general—and recall Najim's observation that military rank is percieved as more respected than civil rank—Najim was typically introduced simply as a mayor from Iraq. I knew him for months before beginning to understand how much more there is to him and his story.

On February 8, 2013, MG McMaster addressed participants in a NESA seminar in Washington, DC. Najim was most pleased to introduce him, as follows:

Men born of the same womb are brothers through the accident or coincidence of birth. But brothers forged in the crucible of battle, tempered in mutual trust and mutual dependence, become lifelong brothers in trial by fire.

In war and in peace, I have been honored to know and serve with many honorable men, men wise and courageous. In the battle to save the city of Tal Afar, long a safe haven and base of operations for al-Qaeda, a friendship grew between former enemies.

Standing shoulder to shoulder in that battle, our friendship deepened in mutual trust and respect, until now, calling him my friend is not honest; it does not say enough. In battle, we became brothers, brothers of different mothers.

I have known wise men, courageous men. But this man's wisdom and courage surpass that of anyone else I have known. I have seen him calm in pitched battle against terrorists. Amid the chaos of war, as even brave men's hearts weakened, his decisiveness, his quiet confidence and reassuring smile, strengthened the hearts and resolve of his troops, giving them the strength and the will to be heroes.

His strength gave strength to them. His confidence and the power of his personality and intellect strengthened their commitment and inspired them to victory.

Major General–then Colonel–H.R. McMaster, understood that winning a war requires more than weapons and technology. He understood that the power of conquering hearts and minds is greater and more enduring than the power of military might. He brought together the rival Shi'ite and Sunni parties to resolve their differences through dialogue instead of violence. He brought justice to the violent and troubled city of Tal Afar.

Realizing that allies needed more than military victory, that they needed the tools to remain strong in the continuing battle against terrorists, he was the first American commander to have his troops work side by side with Iraqi nationals, symbolizing partnership in their mutual quest.

He denied the terrorists the resources they needed and dismantled their support system. He denied them the safe haven they had so long enjoyed in Tal Afar.

Thousands of citizens of Tal Afar recall the contributions of

Gen. McMaster and the 3rd Armored Cavalry Regiment in making flowers sprout from the fear, despair, and death that had so long been all that the citizens of that city had known. He brought hope and smiles to the children of Tal Afar, who had known only fear and hopelessness. To this day, they remember and honor him, and they continue to ask about him

Gen. McMaster changed the image of Americans in the eyes of many Iraqis. Compare his success in driving the insurgents from Tal Afar with minimal damage and loss of life to the widespread destruction and great loss of life in Fallujah. His wisdom and his humanity laid the foundation for U.S. forces to end the massacres and civil war that was being waged throughout Iraq.

Gen. McMaster returned the American forces to the right track when it had veered off course. He conducted military operations like a maestro, leading U.S. and Iraqi forces with surgical precision to remove the malignant tumor that threatened the continued existence of the ancient city of Tal Afar.

There is an Arabic saying about evaluating the worth of man against his weight in gold. By that measure, Gen. H.R. McMaster is indeed a national treasure.

Many leaders, military and civilian, have been honored for their accomplishments. None deserves greater love and respect than my friend—my brother—Major General H.R. McMaster.

Ten Years Later

Najim has returned to Iraq, leaving his family in the United States. Apparently his work—his legacy in clearing Tal Afar, once an al-Qaeda stronghold of terrorists—did not go unnoticed. In 2015 he returned to active duty in the Iraqi Army, at the behest of the Iraqi prime minister. He is serving as the commander of Iraqi troops rooting DAESH out of Nineveh Province.

About the Authors

Iraqi Major General **Najim Abed al-Jubouri** served as an Air Defense intelligence officer under Saddam Hussein. Following the dissolution of the Iraqi Army in 2003, MG al-Jubouri was asked to serve as police chief in the city of Tal Afar in Nineveh Province, when that lawless city was a terrorist haven and stronghold firmly under the control of al-Qaeda.

When the mayor of Tal Afar was discovered to be closely allied with the terrorist network. Najim was asked to serve as mayor as well as police chief. In that dual role, Najim worked closely with American forces to root out al-Qaeda and make Tal Afar a safe and flourishing city again. When al-Qaeda targeted the general and his family, and after he was targeted for assassination, his family threatened and his house blown up, American military friends helped him and his family to emigrate to the United States where they were granted sanctuary.

In late 2008. MG al-Jubouri, usually called "Mayor," became a distinguished researcher at the Near East South Asia (NESA) Center for Strategic Studies in Washington, DC. At NESA, one of the defense department's five regional centers, the mayor lectured, directed seminars, and published papers on Iraqi issues.

In 2015, the Mayor returned to Iraq, when Prime Minister Haider al-Abadi appointed him commander of the forces fighting DAESH (ISIS) in Nineveh Province.

Craig Lancto is a veteran writer and editor who served as deputy chief of outreach and director of communications and media relations at the Near East South Asia Center for Strategic Studies, where he and Najim became colleagues and friends.

When Mr. Lancto retired in 2012, the two decided to collaborate on telling the story of Najim and the city of Tal Afar.

Craig Lancto

craiglanct@gmail.com

By Craig Lancto

Available from Amazon.com

Fighting Ghosts and Chasing the Wind:
The Hero of Tal Afar

What Do You Do for a Sucking Lip Wound?

Alexandria, Virginia: Where History Lives

Banned Books: How Schools Restrict the Reading of
Young People (Published by The World & I)

Baptism: Gateway to New Life?

In and Around the Town of Shenandoah

Reflections on the Shenandoah (Images)

Newspaper-Education Materials
Available through Teachers Pay Teachers
https://www.teacherspayteachers.com/My-Products

Learning Language through the Newspaper

Using the Newspaper for Character Education

Using the Newspaper to Learn, Prefixes, Suffixes,
and Word Roots

Using the Newspaper to Identify Active and
Passive Voice

138

Using the Newspaper to Identify Independent and Dependent Clauses

Using the Newspaper to Identify Simple Sentences

Also from Teachers Pay Teachers

A Guide to Elections, Politics, and Government

Oral History Project

Thanksgiving: a Time to Give Thanks

Powhatan, Pocahontas, and John Smith

World of Work: Interviewing

Romance at Short Notice: Writing a Personal Tale of Adventure

Generating a Lifetime of Writing Ideas

Autobiography or Obituary: What a Difference a Day Makes!

Progressive Prewriting: Developing Writing Ideas

Publishing a Class Book